THE ERRACHT FEUD

*Internal Divisions in
Clan Cameron 1567-77*

THE ERRACHT FEUD

*Internal Divisions
in Clan Cameron
1567-77*

*John Thor Ewing

Commander of Clan Ewing*

WELKIN BOOKS

First Published 2016
Welkin Books Ltd

Copyright © Thor Ewing 2016
Thor Ewing asserts his right to be identified as author and illustrator in accordance with the Design, Copyrights and Patents Act 1988

All rights reserved. No part of this publication may be reproduced, stored in a retrieval system, or transmitted in any form or by any means, without the prior written permission of the publisher, nor be otherwise circulated in any from of binding or cover other than that in which it is published and without a similar condition being imposed upon the subsequent purchaser.

ISBN 978-1-910075-05-0

To Donald Cameron of Lochiel XXVII
Chief of Clan Cameron
in appreciation of his interest and encouragement
in my attempt to rewrite this part
of his family history.

Acknowledgements

My own interest in the Erracht Feud was sparked by my research into the McEwen name, specifically as a tangent to my commentary on the work of R. S. T. MacEwen which has also been published this year. To some extent, I probably owe an acknowledgement to everyone involved in that research, but I will confine my thanks here to those who have been directly connected with this project: Professor Jane Dawson, Dr Martin MacGregor, Alison Diamond, Diane Baptie and Bob Crook. Publication of the Bond of Manrent from the *Argyll Transcripts* on p79 is by kind permission of the Duke of Argyll.

An earlier and briefer draft of the text was submitted for publication in *The Proceedings of the Society of Antiquaries of Scotland*, but it became clear that it would be impossible to fully develop the research within the limited scope of a journal article. The final text has nonetheless benefitted from the anonymous review process it underwent, and I am grateful both to my reviewers and to Erin Osborne-Martin and Dr Vasiliki Koutrafouri for their assistance.

I must also thank my family, who have endured my fascination with this particular decade in Clan Cameron's history with only mild bemusement.

Contents

I. Historical context and past perspectives   9

II. Reassessing the Erracht Feud   20

Notes   54

Appendix I. Key sources and abstracts   62

Appendix II. The Five Arrows of Clan Cameron   83

Bibliography   90

Index   96

Illustrations:
Fig.1. Map showing key locations in Cameron territory, Lochaber. 8
Fig.2. Genealogical table showing kinship between the principal figures in the Erracht Feud.   23

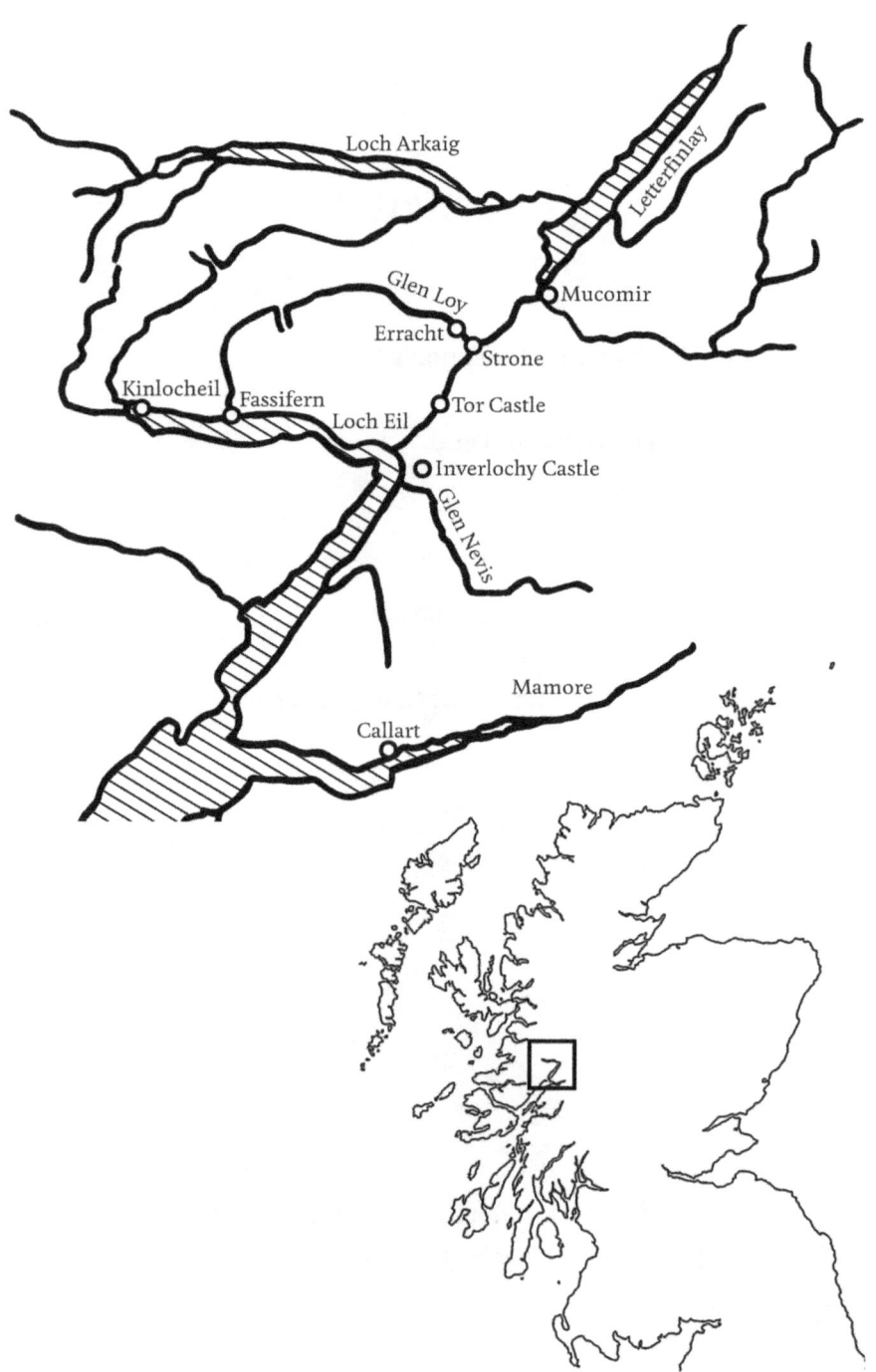

Fig.1. Map showing key locations in Cameron territory, Lochaber.

I

Historical context and past perspectives

IN 1567 the surrender of Mary Queen of Scots at the Battle of Carberry Hill marked the start of the conflict known as the Marian Civil War. Not for the first time, Scots found themselves at odds over who had the right to rule them as a nation. But although this drama dominated the national stage, the dynastic affairs of the monarchy were beyond the horizons of many contemporaries. While the nation as a whole was engaged in warfare between the queen and proponents of her infant son, Clan Cameron was preoccupied with a power struggle of its own between rival scions of the chiefly line.

Like so much in histories of the clans, the details of the Erracht Feud which overtook the Camerons have been overlaid with legend. Traditional stories concerning this episode are fascinating in themselves and can provide useful information towards reconstructing the past, but they are also highly coloured by their particular perspective and indeed they are sometimes entirely misleading. Even among historians, the course of events has been regularly misunderstood, and the protagonists misidentified.

Because of this, a straightforward narrative approach is not possible—there are layers of mistaken history to unpeel before we can tell the true story of the feud. To reach a fresh understanding of the nature of the Erracht Feud and its protagonists, we must proceed by careful analysis and reappraisal of both oral tradition and historical documents, and must draw on new evidence from contemporary sources which has previously been disregarded.

Clan Cameron before 1567

Before turning to older accounts of the feud itself, it is necessary to review the background to the struggle, through the careers of the Cameron chiefs.[1]

Ewen McAllan XIII (c.1480—1546)

The XIIIth chief of Clan Cameron was Ewen, known as Allanson or McAllan after his father Allan Cameron.[2] Ewen McAllan Cameron probably succeeded to the chiefship in around 1480, when his father was killed in a raid against Clan Mackintosh. As chief of Clan Cameron, Ewen became *pater familias* and would have been expected to act as military leader and protector of his people. At this time, the Cameron chiefs seem to have held no lands directly from the Crown, but their clan had traditionally occupied land in Lochaber for which they owed allegiance to their superiors, the MacDonald Lords of the Isles. This bond of allegiance was maintained both through kinship (Ewen's mother Mariot was daughter of Angus MacDonald of the Isles) and through grants of land.

In 1492, Alexander MacDonald of Lochalsh granted various lands to Ewen McAllan, including lands at Loch Eil, confirming the alliance between Camerons and MacDonalds; it was perhaps at around this time that Ewen married Alexander's sister. The very next year, after a long period of political turmoil, King James IV declared the forfeiture of the MacDonald Lordship of the Isles on charges of treason. However, the grant of land at Loch Eil was eventually confirmed by royal charter, and it is by their traditional title of 'Lochiel' that the chiefs of Clan Cameron are known to this day.

Royal power remained relatively weak in the regions which had formed the fiefdom of the MacDonalds. Instead of direct rule, the Crown relied on powerful nobles to act as its agents, principally the

Earls of Argyll, Chiefs of Clan Campbell in the west, and the Earls of Huntly, Chiefs of the Gordons in the north. These two powers now vied with each other for control over the clans and territories which had previously owed allegiance to the MacDonald Lords of the Isles. On the new political map, Cameron lands in Lochaber lay at the midpoint where the realms of influence of Argyll and Huntly met.

Ewen McAllan remained loyal to his kindred and former overlords, supporting the rebellion of Donald Dow MacDonald in 1503, and transferring his allegiance to James MacDonald of Duniveg whom he considered to be 'narrest of Ayr to the hous of the Ylies' after Donald's death.[3] Under his chiefship, Camerons fought repeatedly alongside Clan Donald against Frasers and Grants until, in 1546, Ewen McAllan was apprehended by the combined authority of the Earl of Huntly, Lieutenant of the North, and the Chief of Clan Mackintosh, Steward of Lochaber; he was then tried and beheaded as a rebel.

Ewen Beg McConnell XIV (1546—53)

Clan chiefships did not always descend according to straightforward primogeniture (to the eldest surviving son of the last chief), but often through an ancient Gaelic system known as 'tanistry' by which it was possible for a chief to designate a chosen heir or 'tanist' (Gaelic, *tànaiste*) among several eligible candidates.[4] When Ewen McAllan of Lochiel's eldest son Donald had died in 1538, one might have expected the next-in-line to have been his second son Ewen McEwen Cameron of Erracht. However when Lochiel was executed in 1546, he was succeeded as XIVth chief by his grandson (eldest son of his eldest son) Ewen Beg McConnell Cameron of Lochiel.[5]

The new chief, Ewen Beg McConnell XIV, had a son Donald by the daughter of John MacDougall of Dunollie, Chief of Clan Dougall. According to a tradition recorded in the *Memoirs of Sir Ewen Cameron of Locheill*,[6] Ewen Beg McConnell steadfastly refused to marry the boy's mother, as a result of which he was imprisoned by John MacDougall at Innis Chonnell in Loch Awe, and was killed in 1553 during an abortive rescue attempt led by his own foster-father Martin McConaghy MacMartin of Letterfinlay.[7]

There are difficulties with this tradition, which perhaps suggest the historical narrative has been rewritten in the light of later events. Whilst Innis Chonnell might originally have been a MacDougall possession, from at least the early fourteenth century it had been a seat of Campbell power. After the Earls of Argyll moved to Inveraray, Innis Chonnell was indeed used as a prison, but by the Campbells and not by the MacDougalls of Lorne.[8] Thus, although the tradition of Ewen Beg McConnell's imprisonment at Innis Chonnell may be plausible in itself, the surrounding narrative concerning the mother of Donald McEwen Beg and the implication of his illegitimacy (which is used in the *Memoirs* to discredit his role in the coming feud) is open to suspicion.[9]

Donald Dow McConnell XV (1553-69)

Ewen Beg McConnell was succeeded by his brother Donald Dow McConnell, who thus became XVth chief of Clan Cameron. The new chief married Una, the daughter of Hector Mor Maclean of Duart, Chief of Clan Maclean, and she bore him a son Allan who, in the course of time, would emerge as victor in the feud that was about to envelop the clan.[10]

The period of Donald's chiefship is more-or-less overlooked in most accounts of the clan, but is considered below (p21-31).

Traditional accounts of the Erracht Feud

Drummond of Balhaldie

The most important narrative of the Erracht Feud was recorded in the early eighteenth century in the manuscript of the *Memoirs of Sir Ewen Cameron of Locheill* as part of an 'introductory account' relating the stories of earlier chiefs. The author of the *Memoirs* was John Drummond of Balhaldie, whose mother Margaret was the eldest daughter of Sir Ewen Cameron of Lochiel, and his account may be taken to represent the traditions of the family of Cameron of Lochiel.

According to Balhaldie, the feud 'proceeded ... from the ill conduct and ambition' of two tutors appointed to look after the affairs of the new chief Allan McConnell Dow XVI until he came of age. He names these tutors as 'Donald and John Camerons, two of the younger sones of the famous Ewen McAllan, grand-uncles to the minor, and the predecessors of the Familys of Errocht and Kenlochiell'. However, the 'intolerable insolence and cruelty' of the tutors led the clan to call home Donald McEwen Beg, 'the bastard sone of him that was killed in the Isle of Lochow', which led in turn to 'a kind of civil war' in which both tutors were killed—Donald was 'barbarously murdered' in a meeting of the clan at Inverlochy Castle, while John was 'beheaded at Dunstaffnage'. Finally, Donald McEwen Beg was also killed when the rightful heir, Allan McConnell Dow, returned to reclaim his chiefship.

The *Memoirs* present the feud as a three-cornered struggle. Their account is heavily biased towards Allan, as we should expect from a tradition preserved and transmitted by his descendants, and is unsympathetic towards the other parties to the feud. Balhaldie calls Donald McEwen Beg 'the bastard', referring to his supposed illegitimacy every time he appears in the text, and even citing

Donald's claim that 'he was no bastard, but the sone of a lawfull marriage' among the crimes which help justify his death at the hands of Allan McConnell Dow of Lochiel. Given that our evidence for this claim of illegitimacy is based solely on this text, and the episode which relates to his birth has already been seen to be suspect, we may justifiably doubt Balhaldie's authority on this point.

Balhaldie invariably refers to the leaders of the opposite faction as the 'tutors' of Allan McConnell Dow. Although in common enough use on both sides of the border, the word 'tutor' has different meanings in English and Scots, and is defined in *A Dictionary of the Older Scottish Tongue (up to 1700)* as 'a guardian who is the legal administrator, or one of a group of administrators, of the estate of a minor, failing the father … Also applied to the guardian(s) of a ruler in minority.' This is the sense in which it is used by Balhaldie and in other Scottish documents of the era.

Balhaldie's purpose is to depict a clan at odds with itself, to which only the rightful chief can restore order. He apparently believed Allan's tutors had in some way overstepped their legitimate role, and he alleges corruption and mismanagement. However, his consistent use of the term 'tutor' suggests they did in fact continue to serve their young chief, and although he criticises the Tutors for acting 'more like proprietors than administrators', he acknowledges that they were fulfilling their duty 'during the minority of the Chief.'

His account is clearly confused in identifying the tutors as Donald and John, sons of Ewen McAllan, the XIIIth chief, since Ewen McAllan's eldest son Donald had died in 1538 and was in fact the father of the XIVth and XVth chiefs. Many later historians have based their understanding of the feud almost entirely on this account, usually mediated through the work of Donald Gregory who trustingly relayed it as history.

Mary MacKellar

The second traditional account was set down more than a century later by the poet Mary MacKellar in a letter to *The Celtic Magazine*.[11] The magazine's editor, Alexander Mackenzie, later used MacKellar's account as the basis for his own description of the feud in his *History of the Camerons*.[12] Mary MacKellar drew on Cameron oral traditions which were not merely sympathetic to Donald McEwen Beg, but often adulatory in tone. This seemingly confirms Balhaldie's implication that Donald McEwen Beg had enjoyed popular support. Mary MacKellar's account is not always consistent with Balhaldie's, and sometimes outspokenly contradicts the earlier account. Elsewhere, she has tried to reconcile her own traditions with Balhaldie's account of Lochiel tradition, which had been published in 1842, and she claims that 'each item in [her account] is confirmed by the different histories of those stormy times'.

MacKellar's principal interest (or that of her oral sources) was in traditions concerning Donald McEwen Beg, whom she calls *an Taillear Dubh na Tuaighe*, 'the Black Tailor of the Axe'. She writes that he was dubbed *Taillear*, because as a baby he had been put to nurse with a tailor's wife, where he 'grew up to be a brave and wise man, famous for his powers of sarcasm and ready wit, but more so for the skill with which he wielded his battle-axe, the great weapon of the warriors of Lochaber.' MacKellar had clearly encountered the Lochiel tradition that he was illegitimate but, although she does not wish to challenge this traditional authority, she raises the possibility that his parents were 'handfasted according to the custom of the time', which would invariably have counted as marriage for his contemporaries.[13]

MacKellar's stories portray the young warrior as a free agent, as the hero of the clan, and indeed as a potential chief. Her hagiographic characterisation of Allan McConnell Dow's charismatic cousin contrasts with (and also helps explain) the mixture of hostility and grudging respect with which he is treated in the Lochiel account, but might also suggest that MacKellar's own branch of the clan, *Sliochd Iain Duibh*, had supported Donald McEwen Beg rather more enthusiastically than it supported Allan of Lochiel. However, MacKellar sees no contradiction between support for these two protagonists, as her account interprets Donald McEwen Beg as the saviour and protector of the future chief.

These stories, which show Donald McEwen Beg taking a leading role in clan affairs, presumably relate to a time when his uncle Donald Dow McConnell, the XVth chief, was either dead or in captivity, which is consistent with the Lochiel tradition that Donald McEwen Beg was 'called home' by opponents of the tutors. Yet, in contrast to the Lochiel account, where Allan is rescued from his tutors by his nurse and whisked away to his mother's Maclean kinsfolk on the Isle of Mull, MacKellar's account portrays Allan as a helpless baby at home in the house of his Mackintosh mother.

Mary MacKellar believed that Allan McConnell Dow XVI was not in fact the son of the previous chief, Donald Dow McConnell, but of a younger brother, John Dow McConnell (she uses the Gaelic form 'Iain Dubh'), whom she says was ancestor of the line known as *Sliochd Iain Duibh*.[14] This line however is generally supposed to be descended from John Dow McEwen of Kinlochiel,[15] and MacKellar's association of John Dow, progenitor of *Sliochd Iain Duibh*, with Drumsallie (Gaelic, *Druim-na-Saille*) confirms this identification. Without evidence to the contrary, we must prefer Balhaldie's Lochiel tradition here, which is closer to the events both in date and in that Balhaldie's own mother was great-granddaughter of Allan Cameron of Lochiel. Furthermore, there exists an entry in the *Register of the Privy Seal* which refers to 'the decease of Donald Dow McConnell McKene or

Camrum in 1569' and names his heir as 'Alan Dow McConell Makkene or Camrun, son of the said Donald'.[16]

MacKellar's traditions may possibly have confused the young chief Allan McConnell Dow with a younger cousin, who was the son or grandson of John Dow McConnell. If so, the stories might actually contain genuine historical traditions, but would relate to Donald McEwen Beg's relationship with a future chieftain of *Sliochd Iain Duibh* rather than with the future chief of Clan Cameron.

Although traditional accounts may be one-sided and partisan, the bias which continues to pervade oral narratives even after hundreds of years can reflect the passions and politics of the original feud, and this in itself is evidence for the history of the original events which the sources describe. Mary MacKellar's account is full of vivid details of the life of Donald McEwen Beg which are interesting in their own right and which, whilst it may be true they are sometimes little more than 'ridiculous fables'[17] still preserve a palpable sense of the enthusiasm which must have surrounded her hero in his lifetime. Moreover, these traditional narratives highlight the significance of events which might not be immediately obvious from other sources; contemporary documents are rarely framed as historical accounts, and are often incomprehensible without reference to narrative traditions. Thus, if we do not confront the traditional accounts as sources for critical analysis, we will inevitably absorb them unwittingly through the interpretations of other historians.

Earlier historians

The Erracht Feud has been considered in the past by several historians, notably Donald Gregory, Alexander Mackenzie and John Stewart of Ardvorlich. Mackenzie differs from the rest by favouring the traditions of Mary MacKellar over Balhaldie, but the pattern of all these histories is broadly similar and is established by Gregory who effectively reiterates the account of John Drummond of Balhaldie with one significant alteration; when he comes to the names of the tutors and to the murder at Inverlochy Castle, the name of the victim is altered from Donald to 'Ewin of Erracht'.[18]

Gregory was clearly attempting to make sense of a genuine problem in the Lochiel account, whereby the tutors are named as the brothers Donald and John, but are also said to be the sons of Ewen McAllan whose eldest son Donald had long since died in 1538. Faced with this obvious error, Gregory silently emended the name of the elder tutor to 'Ewin', but in so doing he overlooked the possibility that it is the name 'Donald' which is correct and the father's identity which is mistaken. Gregory must also have been unaware of evidence that Ewen's brother John had in fact been killed in 1550. Through this false substitution the already tangled tale of the Erracht feud took another unnecessary twist.

Thus, according to all previous historians, Allan's two tutors were Ewen McEwen of Erracht and his brother John Dow McEwen of Kinlochiel. Ewen is supposed to have asserted his own claim to the chiefship after he had arranged the assassination of the XVth chief Donald McConnell of Lochiel, his nephew, for which crime he was himself assassinated in 1570.[19]

However, Ewen McEwen of Erracht would probably have been in his seventies when these events took place. In his younger days, when he might have pursued the chiefship more vigorously had he so wished, he had twice stood aside to allow younger kinsmen of Lochiel to become chief. For Ewen suddenly and ruthlessly to seek his own advancement to the chiefship at such a great age would have involved a remarkable *volte face*.

If the identification of one of the tutors as Ewen McEwen of Erracht seems implausible, the identification of the other as John Dow McEwen of Kinlochiel may actually be impossible, as it seems this John Dow McEwen had long since been killed by his second cousin, the XIVth chief Ewen Beg McConnell. An entry in the *Justiciary Court Book* for 27 September 1550 accuses 'Eugenius McDonald McEwin, Captain of Glencamroune' among others of the cruel slaughter of 'John Dow McEwin *alias* Camroune' who is identified by Ardvorlich as John Dow McEwen of Kinlochiel.[18] Clearly, if John Dow McEwen of Kinlochiel was killed in 1550, he cannot have been tutor to Allan McConnell Dow of Lochiel who was not born until c.1562, and he cannot have been responsible for the death of the XVth chief Donald McConnell of Lochiel in 1569.

These problems stem directly from Donald Gregory's interpretation of the Lochiel tradition, by which he assumed that the tutors, who are named by Balhaldie as 'Donald and John Camerons' must in fact have been Ewen and John. In fairness to Gregory, he was guided in this by Balhaldie's statement that the tutors were 'two of the younger sones of the famous Ewen McAllan, grand-uncles to the minor, and the predecessors of the Familys of Errocht and Kenlochiell', but both this statement and Gregory's subsequent renaming of the tutors, would seem to be mistaken.

None of the surviving documents relating to the Erracht Feud refers to the Camerons of Kinlochiel, while all references to the Camerons of Erracht are confined to Ewen's two sons, Donald and John. It would seem therefore, that at some time before Balhaldie set down his account of the traditions of the Camerons of Lochiel, a confusion had arisen between Ewen and John Dow, sons of Ewen McAllan of Lochiel on the one hand, and Donald and John Dow, sons of Ewen McEwen of Erracht on the other. In trying to resolve the problem, the nineteenth-century historian Donald Gregory jumped the wrong way, and later historians have blindly followed suit. Because the main protagonists were misidentified, previous historians have based their analysis of the feud on an entirely false understanding of the events. To understand the true course of events and to begin to assess their significance, we must start afresh drawing on the full range of available evidence.

II

Reassessing the Erracht Feud

Written sources for sixteenth-century clan politics are sometimes scanty but, unlike oral narratives which are subject to change as they pass between the generations, they contain only the errors they had when first written down. When it comes to the Erracht Feud, there is in fact a surprising wealth of contemporary written evidence, some of which has not previously been considered in this context. Drawing on all the various sources, both historical and traditional, it is possible to reach a clearer understanding of what actually happened and why.

The chiefship of Donald Dow McConnell of Lochiel XV

Although it lasted for 16 years, no traditional account survives for the chiefship of Donald Dow McConnell XV and, as a consequence, he has not attracted the attention of historians. Even in Balhaldie's narrative history of the clan, Donald himself is barely mentioned in the entry devoted to his chiefship except to excuse him for his late arrival before the Battle of Corrichie in 1562 where he fought for the queen against the rebel Earl of Huntly,[20] and this omission may well reflect a deliberate decision to draw a veil over an episode in Cameron history. There are however several references in historical documents, which together allow us to piece together a picture of the career of Donald Dow McConnell which, if not complete in all its details, is nonetheless revealing.

It may have been as a reward for his support against Huntly at the Battle of Corrichie that Donald Dow McConnell was granted the lands of Letterfinlay, Stronaba and Lindally.[22] These are the lands of the MacMartins, long-standing allies of the Camerons, and had once belonged to Donald Dow's father Donald McEwen, but had been forfeited when Ewen McAllan was attainted for treason and regranted to the Earl of Huntly. With Huntly's own attainder, they had now come full circle.

We next hear of Donald Dow McConnell in November 1564, when he was involved in a dispute with the MacSorlies of Glennevis. Although originally descended from Clan Donald, this family, like the MacMartins, had become closely associated with Clan Cameron and would eventually take the Cameron name.[23] The MacSorlies were represented by Sorley McConnell VcAllan, Tutor of Glennevis, on behalf of Alastair McAlastair, the infant heir. It seems that Donald Dow McConnell had attempted to commandeer the MacSorlie lands of Mamore and Glen Nevis, and to take young Alastair's inheritance for himself.[24] Donald lost his case and, during the proceedings, was briefly confined to Edinburgh by order of the Privy Council. There may have been more to the affair than a polite verbal disagreement over title, and Donald Dow McConnell was compelled to swear that he would 'keip guid rewll and ordour in the cuntre, and on na wyis molest, troubill, nor inquiet ony of our Soverane Ladiis liegis, in bodiis or gudis, be force and way of deid, utherwyise nor be ordour of law and justice', and his uncle John Grant of Freuchie stood surety for him on pain of the princely sum of 2,000 marks.[25] Had Donald Dow succeeded in making the MacSorlies his feudal dependents like the MacMartins, he would have gained a hold over them which might have ensured their continuing loyalty, but his failed attempt to achieve this can have bred only discontent.

At the time of the Chase-About Raid in 1565, when Argyll supported the Earl of Moray's rebellion against the queen, the Camerons in Rannoch seem to have been raided by Grey Colin

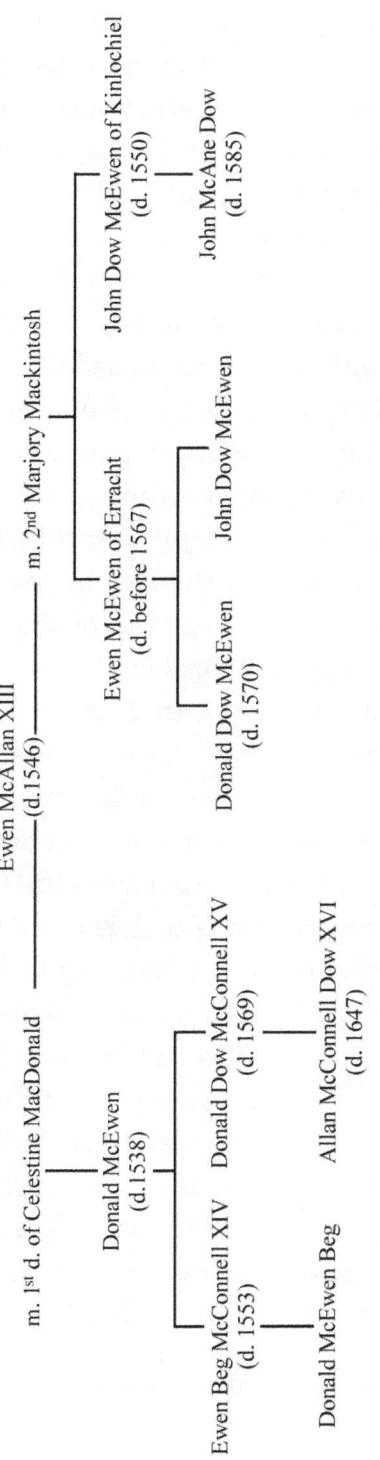

Fig.2. Genealogical table showing kinship between the principal figures in the Erracht Feud.

Campbell of Glenorchy. We may guess that Donald Dow McConnell had sided with Atholl and the queen against Argyll, and that this raid was intended to punish the clan. Whatever the background, it was an affront to Cameron honour and, in September 1565, Ranald Og MacDonald of Keppoch warned Glenorchy that 'als to the Clancamron thai gadderit to revenge this last harschipe that wos doun in Rannoch in to sum plece on yow'.[26] It seems that in the end, Lochiel backed down and, in January 1566 or thereabouts, he wrote to 'my speciale frend Collyne Campbell off Glenorquhay' that 'I knaw nocht in quhat punctis I have offendit yow' and that 'I suld be reddy with all my mycht tow do yow guid service'.[27] But Glenorchy knew that, despite his protestations of loyal service and his appeal to a bond of 'guid nychtborsschepe', Donald Dow McConnell was dealing with the queen and the Earl of Atholl. On 13 February, Glenorchy wrote that 'the capitane of Clanchamrone' was in Edinburgh with Stewart of Appin, MacDonald of Clanranald and an ambassador from Maclean of Duart. They had brought the symbolic gift of a musket, a sword and a 'dager of the Erland fassioun' to inform the queen and Atholl 'that the Queene wyll get all the men of the Ylis to tak part with hir in contrar my Lord of Argyll'.[28]

At some point in this conflict, Glenorchy had taken prisoners from the Camerons of Erracht. Usually, they could have expected their chief to speak for them as their protector, so it is interesting that in March 1566 the appeal for their release is made not by Donald Dow McConnell of Lochiel but directly by 'clane Ewyn WcEwyn' (i.e. Donald Dow and John Dow McEwen of Erracht).[29] It's intriguing that it is the family of Erracht rather than Lochiel which takes this action and that no special explanation is given in the letter, suggesting that the McEwen Camerons of Erracht may already have been perceived as potential alternative clan leaders by local magnates, and this might hint at emerging tensions within Clan Cameron.[30] The fact that William Stewart does not refer to Ewen McEwen himself but to his 'clan' probably indicates that Ewen was already dead by this date.

When Donald Dow McConnell had offered support for the queen against Argyll, he may have hoped for a particular reward which was in her gift. The clan lands of the Camerons in Glen Loy and Loch Arkaig had been forfeited when Ewen McAllan Cameron XIII was denounced as a traitor, but had not been formally regranted since the death of William Mackintosh in 1550. These lands had anciently belonged to the ancestors of Clan Cameron, but had been a cause of contention with Clan Mackintosh since the Battle of Drumlui in 1337, and came to be known as the 'Disputed Lands'.

The queen would use the promise of lands and titles as an enticement to her subjects. Thus, when in 1565, she offered lands in Breadalbane to Gregor Roy MacGregor of Glenstrae if he would join herself and Atholl against Argyll, the Earl of Argyll commented wryly to Glenorchy that 'that will in na wayis move him for we knaw that the erledom of Ergyll wald be promisit to yow or sum uther of our freindis in lik maner for the lyk service gif it wald be acceptit'.[31] But if possession of the Disputed Lands was the reward which Donald Dow McConnell hoped to gain by going against Argyll, he would be disappointed. On 14th June 1567, just one day before her surrender to the Confederate Lords at Carberry Hill, the queen signed a Crown Precept of Sasine by which Lachlan Mackintosh was served heir to the lands of Glen Loy and Loch Arkaig. In her own crisis, Mary looked for support to Huntly, whose father she had defeated at the Battle of Corrichie with the support of Donald Dow McConnell. Lachlan Mackintosh was among Huntly's most trusted and powerful supporters, and it was he who now reaped the reward. Quite possibly, Mackintosh's inheritance had been deliberately delayed in order to keep Donald Dow McConnell on side.[32]

The queen's decision to grant the Disputed Lands to Lachlan Mackintosh may have owed as much to Donald Dow McConnell's bad luck as to his bad judgement, but it must still have been a major blow to his authority as chief. Perhaps more important than the symbolic history of contention over Glen Loy and Loch Arkaig was the simple fact that these lands were home to a large part of his clan. Henceforth, they would occupy their lands only as feudal dependents of another clan. It could be seen as the final failure of a policy, which had made powerful enemies in Glenorchy and Argyll, and had apparently won him nothing in return.

In June 1567, Mary Queen of Scots was imprisoned at Lochleven Castle where, one month later, she was forced to abdicate. Any hope of royal favour was now gone. Donald Dow McConnell had committed his clan to the support of a fallen queen and the Catholic Earl of Atholl, but the country was now ruled by her opponents, the Protestant Lords of the Congregation, in the name of her infant son.

26 December 1567, Donald Dow McEwen of Erracht assumes power

The first documentary evidence connected with the brewing feud in Clan Cameron is a Bond of Manrent by which 'Martyne McDonquhie Vic Martyne' promises to serve 'Donald McEwin Vic Ewin'.[33] A Bond of Manrent was a written record setting out the relationship between a lord and his followers, whereby one man, sometimes as the representative of his kin group or clan, offered loyalty and service on behalf of himself and his kin, in exchange for the protection and leadership of a more powerful chieftain or lord.[34] This Bond affirms the bonds of kinship due between Martin McConaghy, chieftain of the MacMartins of Letterfinlay, and Donald Dow McEwen of Erracht as his new chief and feudal overlord.

The place name Erracht (or *Eireachd*) is Gaelic meaning 'Place of Assembly' and, from the date of the Bond, we may guess that the clan had assembled either here or at nearby Strone for Christmas. Such a gathering was more than an opportunity to renew bonds of kinship and goodwill. The *fine* of the clan, made up of the heads of the leading families, acted as a clan council, and was expected to offer advice and criticism for their chief, and even, if necessary, to replace him.35

This Bond of Manrent bears witness to a momentous meeting. The council has clearly gone badly for the chief Donald Dow McConnell, who is now a prisoner. He has apparently resisted the judgement of his clan against him, and was supported only by his feudal dependent Martin McConaghy. Both men have been seized, and Donald Dow (perhaps along with his brother John Dow) McEwen of Erracht has been appointed as Tutor of Lochiel, making him effective regent on behalf of the young chief Allan McConnell Dow. Donald Dow McEwen has now released Martin McConaghy of Letterfinlay, on condition that he accept Erracht's authority in place of Lochiel's. Lochiel himself remains a prisoner, probably in his own stronghold of Tor Castle, where we must assume Donald Dow McEwen's brother John Dow is his warder.

By this agreement, Donald Dow McEwen takes charge of the lands of the MacMartins as their overlord; Martin McConaghy is free to hold his lands as before, but instead of possessing his lands as a vassal of Lochiel, he now holds them as a vassal of Erracht. Martin's own material position is unaffected by the agreement. He has simply swapped one lord for another.

With this Bond, Donald Dow McEwen established himself as *de facto* chief of Clan Cameron,37 but it is extremely unlikely that the McEwen Camerons of Erracht were acting alone. Instead, a number of leading families within the clan will have chosen to take matters into their own hands, and a consensus built around Donald Dow McEwen of Erracht as a suitable interim leader or regent, to oversee affairs until Allan McConnell Dow could take on the duties of chiefship in his own right. The clan needed strong and effective leadership and, if the existing chief had failed to provide this, then extraordinary measures would have been readily justified.

Neither of the traditional accounts overtly recalls this coup or the captivity of Donald Dow McConnell between 1567 and 1569, but this interpretation of events, whereby Donald Dow McEwen's role as tutor allows him to act as regent for Allan McConnell Dow, is consistent with the story as recounted by Balhaldie. In the absence of criticism in traditional accounts, we must presume that, with a possible exception in the MacMartins of Letterfinlay, the imprisonment of Donald Dow McConnell was broadly accepted or perhaps even welcomed within Clan Cameron.

Martin McConaghy, chieftain of the MacMartins, may have felt an abiding loyalty to his imprisoned former lord, and stipulates in the terms of his Bond that he should be free to serve Donald Dow McConnell of Lochiel again if he has the opportunity. This was the same 'Martin McConnochey of Lattir Finlay' who Balhaldie says had led the raid on Innis Chonnel to free Donald's brother Ewen Beg in 1553.[36] If Martin or his family were to do the same again and free Donald Dow McConnell, the old chief would be able to call on the services of his feudal dependents as lord of Loch Eil and Letterfinlay against the McEwen Camerons of Erracht. It would be all too easy for the Tutors to provoke the enmity of such an unwilling vassal, and this prospect must have made the continuing life of their captive a thorn in the side of Donald Dow and John Dow McEwen.

Donald Dow McConnell was now the prisoner of his clan in Lochaber, while the queen he had served was the prisoner of her nobles in Lochleven. The queen had been forced to abdicate in favour of her infant son and, no doubt, the *fine* of Clan Cameron hoped that the imprisonment of their chief would likewise lead to his abdication in favour of his own son. It seems likely however that Donald Dow McConnell stubbornly refused to play along, and would relinquish neither his chiefship nor his feudal rights.

1569, Death of the XVth chief, Donald Dow McConnell of Lochiel

This impasse was resolved in 1569 with the death of the old chief.[38] Earlier historians have usually assumed that Donald Dow McConnell was assassinated in a bid to secure the chiefship for Erracht,[39] but there is in fact no evidence to suggest that either Donald or John Dow McEwen ever pursued the chiefship on their own behalf. A very different perspective on this killing is offered by analogy with the parallel imprisonment of Mary Queen of Scots. According to a report of 1594, Patrick Lindsay finally extracted Mary's agreement to her abdication only after threatening her life, saying 'that if she did not sign the document she would compel them to cut her throat, however unwilling they might be'.[40]

Donald Dow McConnell would never have been made a prisoner had he not already refused to surrender power. Although his captors would no doubt have preferred his willing capitulation, the old chief was determined to hang on, even in the teeth of opposition from his own clan. In such circumstances, threats must surely have been levelled at Donald Dow McConnell just as they were at Mary Queen of Scots. Mary had ultimately agreed to save her own life through abdication in favour of her son, but if Donald Dow McConnell continued to refuse to cooperate, the threats could only have been repeated, growing less potent with each reiteration until finally John Dow McEwen felt impelled to carry them out.

At the time of the killing, Donald Dow McEwen enjoyed the support of the clan as Tutor of Lochiel, so it was not until 1572 when the feud was at its height that, in what looks like a game of legal tit-for-tat, John Dow McEwen was put to the horn for the murder of Donald Dow McConnell. There is, however, no real reason to doubt that the McEwens of Erracht were responsible for the old chief's death. In a letter of August 1570, in what appears to be the earliest reference to the killing, Donald Dow McEwen wrote that Donald Dow McConnell's uncle John Grant of Freuchie 'hes writin to me that he wes miscontent of the deid that my bruther did last'.[41] This unnamed 'deid' must surely be the killing of Donald Dow McConnell—it seems that, after a year of intransigence on the part of his prisoner, John Dow's patience had finally snapped, but his elder brother Donald was sharply aware of the potential divisiveness of this 'deid' and was keen to dissociate himself from it.

It was apparently the death of the old chief that led to the arrival of a new player at the table. As Balhaldie has it, 'To make head against [the tutors], the opposite faction called home Donald McEwan [Beg]'.[42] Having been summoned to defend the interests of others, he is able to enter the arena of clan politics without the taint of self-interest—*Na sir is na seachain an cath*, 'Not to seek nor to avoid battle' was the rule,[43] and with the arrival of Donald McEwen Beg, *an Taillear Dubh*, a battle would swiftly ensue for control of the clan. Thus it is at this point, not with the appointment of Erracht as Tutor of Lochiel, that the feud actually begins.

At the time of his father's death, Allan McConnell Dow of Lochiel was too young to rule in his own right—he was still a child under the tutelage of Donald Dow McEwen. According to Balhaldie, Allan was sequestered with his Maclean relatives on the Isle of Mull and, in the midst of the turmoil which now enveloped his clan, there would be no prospect of his imminent return.

Balhaldie's account portrays Donald McEwen Beg as the leader of the rebel faction against the rule of the tutors as representatives of Allan McConnell Dow of Lochiel. By contrast, MacKellar suggests instead that it was Donald McEwen Beg who was defending the right of Allan McConnell Dow and that he 'watched over his [Allan's] interests through all the years of his absence'. Reasonably enough, previous historians have tended to agree that, if the McEwens of Erracht killed Donald Dow McConnell, they cannot also have supported his son Allan McConnell Dow.

Paradoxically however, just as the gaolers of the queen were empowered by loyalty to her son, it may have been his very support for the young Allan which led John Dow McEwen to kill the boy's father. Consequently, there is no reason to believe that Donald McEwen Beg was acting on behalf of his cousin Allan McConnell Dow, whose interests continued to be represented by his tutors. Colourful and romantic as her account may be, on this as on so many other points, MacKellar's traditions are apparently unreliable.

1569, Agreement over Glen Loy and Loch Arkaig

With the old chief dead, the McEwens of Erracht were free to fulfil their role as tutors and to strike deals on behalf of their clan. MacFarlane's *Genealogical Collections*[44] contains a note of the contract between Lachlan Mor Mackintosh and Donald and John Dow McEwen of Erracht, by which the Camerons would lease Glen Loy and Loch Arkaig for an annual rent of 80 merks.

These were the so-called 'Disputed Lands' which lay at the heart of a long-running conflict between Clan Cameron and their neighbours of Clan Mackintosh. Although continuing intermarriage at the highest level between the clans shows that the dispute did not always result in bitterness and bloodshed, contention over Glen Loy and

Loch Arkaig had overshadowed Cameron-Mackintosh relations for more than two centuries and had claimed the life of the XIIth Cameron chief in 1480.[45] No doubt this feud was usually expressed in low-level reiving and raiding, but it could erupt into full-blown warfare as it did at the Battle of Drumlui in 1337, the Battle of Invernahavon in 1370 or 1386,[46] and the Battle of Palm Sunday in 1429.[47] The Disputed Lands had been granted to the XIIIth chief, Ewen McAllan Cameron, in 1528, but were lost again when he was executed as a traitor in 1546.[48] Control of the lands of Glen Loy and Loch Arkaig was thus highly symbolic, but the rights of Lachlan Mackintosh over Glen Loy and Loch Arkaig had been confirmed by charter as recently as 1567,[49] and it would have been a desperate act of defiance to continue to claim these lands by *còir claidheimh*, by 'right of the sword'.

Balhaldie believed the deal was imposed by force, and says that Mackintosh 'marched into the country at the head of such a body of men, as the tutors, in their present situation, were unable to resist, and obliged them to submitt to a treaty', but the agreement does not seem particularly one-sided, and even Balhaldie concedes that 80 merks was 'an inconsiderable rent'.[50] In fact, it was rather a good deal for the Camerons—Mackintosh had just paid duty on these lands at three times that rate for the period 1550-67. As close cousins, Lachlan Mackintosh and the McEwens of Erracht might have seen this as an opportunity to seal a friendship between the two clans and put an end to centuries of futile warfare. So, if Mackintosh men did come in strength, it may well have been by invitation.

Nonetheless, by this agreement, the McEwens of Erracht recognised that Mackintosh had the legal right to these lands as their feudal superiors, and so subjected themselves to Mackintosh authority. According to Anne Grant of Laggan, a clan chief was 'not allowed to part with territory [even] for the preservation of his life' and could lose his chiefship if he failed in this duty, as had apparently occurred when Fraser of Lovat lost Abertarff to MacDonald of Glengarry,[51] and local tradition recalled how MacDonald of Keppoch had lost rank both for himself and his clan when he capitulated to Clan Mackintosh in 1498.[52]

The fall of Donald Dow McConnell XV in 1567 can probably be attributed in large part to his failure to gain control of these very lands for himself. Two years on, Donald and John Dow McEwen had undoubtedly made the best of the situation they inherited, but in so-doing they had acknowledged their own inability to restore the lands to Cameron ownership as in the days of their grandfather, Ewen McAllan XIII. So, although the Camerons had no legal title to the Disputed Lands, the recognition of Mackintosh's precedence on such a contentious issue would clearly have been a sufficient pretext for an opposing faction to reject Erracht's authority, or for a determined rival to stir up resentment within the clan.

Clearly, the deal over Glen Loy and Loch Arkaig presented an opportunity for Donald McEwen Beg and, to judge by his traditional reputation (MacKellar writes that he 'hated the Mackintoshes, and nothing pleased him better than to wield his axe against them on the battle-field'), we may suppose that he took full advantage of the situation to embarrass the Erracht faction and further his own cause.

The loss of Glen Loy and Loch Arkaig cannot be blamed on the Erracht McEwens, who simply acknowledged an established political reality. Although the Camerons of Lochiel would once more take control of their clan in the 1570s, they too would ultimately have to reach a deal with Mackintosh over the Disputed Lands.[53] Nevertheless, the dispute over Glen Loy and Loch Arkaig would not be finally resolved for almost another century until the Standoff at the Fords of Arkaig in 1665.[54]

4 April 1570, Contract of mutual defence

A remarkable agreement appears among the 'Charters and Miscellaneous Writs of the Grants of Grant'.[55] The parties to this agreement are all either Camerons or allied families of the same clan who have traditionally followed a single chief, but now find themselves on opposing sides in a conflict between between Donald Dow McEwen and Donald McEwen Beg. The agreement does not prohibit the signatories from taking part in the feud but, in the light of the deepening crisis, they have made a pact of mutual defence whereby they agree to 'fortife, mantein and defend' each other 'contrar all mortale' until they have 'ane lauchfull chief, tutor or curator, quha sall haif the steir and gouernance of thair cuntray of Lochchabir, to the quhilk chief, tutor or curator, tha are bayth contentit to obey'.

Whilst this document may not intensify the feud, it clearly testifies to the growing seriousness of the situation. This is the moment when, according to Balhaldie's account, Donald McEwen Beg's arrival in Lochaber had 'occaisioned a kind of civil war'[56] and the contract is a response to this unrest. It is a form of agreement known in Gaelic as *comh-cheangal* 'a bond of friendship' and, according to Martin Martin, writing in about 1695, it would be 'ratify'd by drinking a Drop of each other's Blood, which was commonly drawn out of the little Finger. This was religiously observ'd as a sacred Bond; and if any Person after such an Alliance happen'd to violate the same, he was from that time reputed unworthy of all honest Mens Conversation'.[57] This custom is recalled in the proverb, *Is milis fuil nàmhaid, ach is milse fuil caraid*, 'An enemy's blood is sweet, but a friend's blood is sweeter'.[58]

The first man named in the Contract, Donald McAllan VcEwen in Mamore, would seem to be the grandson of Ewen McAllan XIII through his illegitimate son Allan McEwen[59] and it is clear that, unlike the other signatories, he supports Donald Dow McEwen of Erracht as Tutor of Lochiel.[60] His home in Mamore is on land owned by the MacSorlies of Glennevis, but might also have put him in uncomfortably close proximity to Donald McEwen Beg, who according to a document of 1582, was also 'in Manmoir'.[61] This contract gives Donald McAllan McEwen the assurance that his disagreement with his neighbour over the chiefship of the clan will not turn into an organised man hunt. The divisive potential of the feud is illustrated in the fact that Donald McAllan's brothers also appear in the Contract, but they are among the 'latter parties' who support Donald McEwen Beg.[62]

The fact that this document has been preserved among the Grant papers confirms that John Grant of Freuchie had indeed intervened in Cameron affairs. John Grant of Freuchie had stood surety for Donald Dow McConnell in 1564 and, as uncle of the old chief, he commanded respect within Clan Cameron. It would seem that he had now lost his patience with the appointed Tutors of Lochiel, and thrown his considerable weight behind a rival claimant for the chiefship, his kinsman Donald McEwen Beg. Both Balhaldie and MacKellar draw attention to Donald McEwen Beg's kinship with Grant, and say that he had lived with him immediately before his return to Lochaber. Grant's involvement on behalf of Donald McEwen Beg is also confirmed in a letter of Donald Dow McEwen, who wrote that 'the Lard of Grant beis in Blair to furthset my freindis materis in my contrar'.[63]

Raiding and reiving, 1570

The cattle raid, *togail creach*, was the commonest form of aggression in the heroic society of the Scottish clans, and one of the principal duties of the chief was to lead his clan in such raids.[64] The first foray of a new chief had a special status affirming his right to rule,[65] but, whereas initially the McEwens of Erracht might have been content to sit tight and act as caretakers until the young Lochiel was ready to lead in his own right, the situation had been altered by the arrival of a charismatic and energetic rival claimant. To judge from the account of Mary MacKellar, it seems that Donald McEwen Beg was more than ready to lead his followers on daring raids against Clan Mackintosh, and that his reputation grew with each new exploit. The Erracht faction had to offer something to stir the loyalty of their clan, if they were to compete with their new rival.

In a dramatic reversal of Donald Dow McConnell's political alliance with Atholl, in early June 1570 'Ane certan of Clanchamroun' raided Blair in Atholl, taking 'ane gret nummer of guidis' home to Rannoch[66]—there can be little doubt that this was the part of the clan led by Erracht. Although John Stewart, Earl of Atholl was said to be 'nay thyng contentit bot heichle ofendit thairwith', his response was both cautious and moderate. In a letter of 28 June 1570, Atholl writes obliquely to Grey Colin Campbell of Glenorchy of 'the purpoiss that Johane Steuart of the Appin hes schawin yowe concerning the Clan Ewin WikEwin', advising that he should 'spur thame to that affect'—John Stewart of Appin was the future father-in-law of Allan McConnell Cameron of Lochiel, and Balhaldie's account suggests that Allan was already acquainted with his daughter when he travelled to Appin later that year, so Appin's positive intervention in Erracht affairs at this juncture suggests that he still trusted in their good faith as Tutors of Lochiel.[67]

Although not explicitly stated, it is clear that the 'purpose' intended for the McEwens of Erracht was the pursuit of Clan Gregor. After a brief respite in his feud against the MacGregors, Grey Colin Campbell of Glenorchy had recently secured dominance and had executed the MacGregor chief with his own hand. Now, in conjunction with the Earl of Atholl, he meant to press home his advantage and, at Appin's suggestion, he would employ the Camerons to prosecute his feud and, in so-doing, keep them from raiding at random elsewhere. Just a month after their raid on Blair, the Earl of Atholl noted that 'the Clanewin hes promussit . . . to persew the Clangregor to the wttermaist'.[68]

Perhaps unsurprisingly, in view of Clan Cameron's dealings with Glenorchy during the chiefship of Donald Dow McConnell, there was a certain amount of wariness on both sides. The Camerons were worried 'that in cuming throcht your boundis . . . that your serwandis and the Erlls of Argyllis quha ar now put furthe sall do thaim harme',[69] and on 13 July, Grandtully wrote to reassure Glenorchy 'that the Clanchamron suld do yow nay skayth' but 'desyris your assurance to the effect thai may do yow plesuir and nay ewil'. Meanwhile, Ranald MacDonald of Keppoch told Atholl that he was also 'in redinese beith my self and my men quhon evir your Lordship plasis to dissayr me' but was equally worried that they might encounter either the Campbells or the Camerons for 'I heiff ne will that we and the Lord Argyllis men or the Clancameron suld meith wder'.[70] Highland warfare had traditionally been conducted by individual clans for the sake of honour and cattle, and any attempt at co-ordinated action by several independent clans was fraught with dangers, whereby old rivalries could easily have over-ridden new alliances. But despite his concerns, on 13 July, Glenorchy sent an assurance allowing Donald Dow McEwen and his men to pass through his lands in pursuit of the MacGregors.[71]

Glenorchy's misgivings would seem to have proved justified when Donald Dow McEwen led a raid against Strath Fillan, which belonged not to the MacGregors but to Glenorchy's own kinsman, John

Campbell of Lawers. In a letter of 27 July, Argyll observed that the Camerons had plundered for 'luiff of the kye' rather than out of any desire to help Atholl and Grey Colin against Clan Gregor,[72] and Grandtully also wrote that 'the Clanchamroun hes tane up the Laird of Lawaris geir withe sum of his serwandis and slane ane in Straythfillanen'.[73] However, Lawers had recently been less than enthusiatic in his support for Grey Colin's feud with the MacGregors,[74] and Glenorchy himself seems not to have been troubled on his kinsman's behalf.[75]

On 2 August, Donald Dow McEwen wrote to Glenorchy promising 'to contennew in the service that I have beginnyn', adding that, 'I will nocht desist fra pershewing of the Clangregor' and asking 'that your Maister sall revard me and my bruther efferand to our service'.[76] The reward he hoped for may have had to do with internal Cameron affairs, and he points out that it would also serve Glenorchy's interests to reunite the Camerons, 'For ye knaw I ma nocht guidlie pershew the Clangregor to the rigour quhill the[re] be sum ordour put betux me and thais of my kyn that ar with Evyn Beg Soune.' He ends enigmatically, 'The rest of my mynd wer to lang to wrett.'

A week later he wrote again, seemingly in a state of some agitation. In his second letter, Donald seems desperate for a positive intervention from Grey Colin, coming straight to the point in his request, 'Pleis your Master be remembrit wpoun my last wretting to yow and vil God I will contennew in furthfillin of the punctis heirof sua your Mastership vill do the lik in furthfillling of your part towartis me and my bruther'.[77]

Donald's pleas did not fall on deaf ears. Although no letter survives from Colin Campbell of Glenorchy himself, on 11 August 1570 William Maitland of Lethington replied to a letter concerning the case of Donald McEwen of Erracht saying, 'I sall lat him knaw your mynd towart him and the solistatioun of me for his purpois'.[78] Again on 19 October, William Stewart of Grandtully responded to a request from Lady Glenorchy concerning Donald Dow, saying that he should send a man to the Earl of Atholl for a private message of which Atholl 'wald writ nayne'.[79]

15 April 1572, Donald McEwen Beg put to the horn for the death of Donald Dow McEwen of Erracht

A Letter of Gift of 1572 lists 25 Camerons who are denounced and put to the horn, 'at the instance of John Dow McEwin in Lochquhabir, brother of the deceased Donald Dow McEwin, and his remanent kin and friends, for not finding caution to appear in the tolbooth of Leith, and answer for the slaughter of the said Donald'.[80] The list of the guilty parties is headed by Donald McEwen Beg ('Donald McEwin VcOnill') and, among his 24 associates in the killing of Donald Dow McEwen of Erracht, are Martin McConaghy of Letterfinlay, and John Cam and Alastair Dow McAllan of Callart who had all signed the Bond of Friendship in 1570.[81]

Balhaldie tells us that Donald Dow McEwen was 'barbarously murdered' at a meeting of the clan at Inverlochy Castle and that although this meeting was supposed to resolve the differences between the factions, the murder ensured that 'their mutuall resentment and hatred was kindled into greater fury than before'.[82] In the light of the captivity and death of Donald Dow McConnell following the clan council of Christmas 1567, Donald McEwen Beg would hardly have been eager to meet his adversaries at Erracht, and may have suggested Inverlochy as an alternative meeting place. But Inverlochy Castle would not prove to be the neutral ground it may have seemed—Ewen McAne, Captain of Inverlochy, is named second among the accomplices to the murder, followed by the names of his sons, and then his nephews the McAllans of Callart who had earlier put their names to the Contract of Mutual Defence. John and Alastair McAllan would later be captured and denounced as rebels by the Earl of Atholl for the slaughter of 'Donald Dow McKewin'.[83]

After a sudden flurry of references which suggest that he had taken command of the clan in his role as Tutor of Lochiel, Donald Dow McEwen of Erracht does not reappear in the records after October 1570, making a date of Christmas 1570 most likely for his death. It is shortly after this date that John Caddell of Aslowne was made ward of the lands belonging to Lochiel, perhaps indicating that Donald alone had been officially recognised as Tutor of Lochiel.[84]

9 July 1572, John Dow McEwen put to the horn for the death of Donald Dow McConnell of Lochiel (ob.1569)

The Justiciary Court Book records that in 1572, 'Johnne Dow MacKewyne WicKewyn' and others of Clan Cameron were put to the horn for 'art and part of the slaughter of vmqle Donald Dow MacCoule WicEwyn, Captain of Clanranald'.[85] As Ardvorlich points out, this reference to Clanranald makes no sense and it should read 'Captain of Clancameron'.[86]

Coming as it does three years after the event, and less than three months after Donald McEwen Beg has himself been put to the horn for a similar crime, this has the look of a game of legal tit-for-tat. Given too that Balhaldie makes no mention of Donald Dow McConnell's murder, it would seem possible that John Dow McEwen and his followers were framed for a murder which never actually took place. It is more likely however that Balhaldie omitted to mention the murder of Donald Dow McConnell because it raises awkward questions about his chiefship which Balhaldie preferred to leave unanswered. Although Donald Dow McEwen's name would have been omitted from the list of the accused because he too had now been killed, he probably had actually taken no part in the killing, which he refers to in his letter of August 1570 as 'the deid that my bruther did'.[87]

With the leaders of both factions now put to the horn, a period of uneventful stalemate ensued. Neither Donald McEwen Beg nor John Dow McEwen dared risk any impetuous action, so each sat tight as chieftain of his own following. Perhaps Donald McEwen Beg cemented his reputation by continuing to raid Clan Mackintosh, but there is no evidence that John Dow McEwen took any further part in Glenorchy's feud against the MacGregors. There is no documentary reference to either Cameron faction for the next five years, and when at length we do meet them again, it is not in Lochaber but in Argyll.

John Dow McEwen and Donald McEwen Beg offer fealty to Argyll, 1577

In the sixteenth century, following the demise of the MacDonald Lordship of the Isles, the Earls of Argyll successfully established themselves as *Ceannas na nGaoidheal*, Heads of the Gael, and, during the 1570's, Colin Campbell, 6th Earl of Argyll, was taking Bonds of Manrent from all and sundry throughout the Western Highlands and Isles.[88] Among these was a Bond of Manrent of 11 June 1577, which confirmed 'Donald McEwne Vcdonill and Johne dow mcewne vcewine campbronis' as followers of the Earl of Argyll.[89] Each faction may once have hoped for partisan support from Argyll's network of alliances,[90] but with this Bond they jointly submit to his service. It is unclear whether their appearance together here represents a genuine reconciliation, or is simply a matter of political convenience, but the effect was to give overall control of the clan to Argyll, and the back of the paper is enscribed with the words, 'Clan Camerons bond giveing pledge to observe there manrent 1577'.

Whilst both the factional leaders of Clan Cameron now recognised the authority of the Earl of Argyll, it is possible to see the young Allan McConnell Dow as his protégé. When first he fled from Lochaber, the boy Allan had been sent to his uncle Hector Og Maclean on the Isle of Mull for protection.[91] Hector's wife Janet was the sister of Archibald and Colin Campbell, successive earls of Argyll, and they undoubtedly had a hand in Allan's removal to Dunoon, where his education was entrusted to 'Mr John Cameron, Minister of Dunune, his kinsman, and a person of great probity and learning, by whom he was trained up in the Protestant Religion, which then began to gett footing in the Highlands'.[92] For Argyll, this must have seemed a Providential opportunity to establish the seed of Protestantism at the heart of Clan Cameron.

Having taken control of both Cameron factions through the Bond of 1577, it may have been possible for Argyll to ensure the peaceful restoration of Allan McConnell Dow of Lochiel to his clan, making good the boast of the poem *Maith an Chairt Ceannas na nGaoidheal*, 'When [Argyll] has gained each clan's headship he makes a treaty of permanent peace; thenceforth he maintains law and order, dispenses justice by them unthought'.[93] From Argyll's perspective, such a resolution would not only retore unity to Clan Cameron, but would maintain and enhance the order and stability of his own position as Head of the Gael, whilst also benefitting both the Protestant Kirk and the Crown.

Allan Cameron of Lochiel returns to Lochaber, 1578

It was almost certainly in January 1578 that Allan McConnell Dow first took up his hereditary title as chief of Clan Cameron. In a Bond of Assurance which is inexplicably misdated 1557/8,[94] he styles himself as 'Chief and Captain of Clan Chamroun', and signs himself as 'Allane Camrone, Lard Of Locheill'. Allan gives his assurance of peace towards all those who might have reason to fear his enmity, and many of the names addressed in his Bond of Assurance can be recognised as the supporters of Donald McEwen Beg.[95] He also announces his intention to, 'hald Johanne Dow McEvyn sonnis in thair awne rowmis quhill Witsonday sua that the giff me mete and drink resonable as utheris in the cuntreth, and that I sall have the service of thair tennendis that dwellis apon the grund'.[96]

With this assurance, Allan guaranteed the rights of all parties except the McEwens of Erracht and this has been read as evidence that he had opposed and overthrown Erracht rule, but it seems more likely that Allan's assurance of peace was extended only to those who might have had reason either to fear his enmity or mistrust his intentions. As his loyal supporters, the Camerons of Erracht had no need of such an assurance. Likewise, it is precisely because of the established loyalty of the sons of John Dow McEwen that Allan could so confidently assert his authority over them.

Lochiel's assurance of peace allows his clan the opportunity to reunite behind its new leader. The inclusion of Lachlan Mackintosh in the Bond of Assurance indicates that Allan's initial policies probably continued those pursued by his tutors, Donald and John Dow McEwen of Erracht, whereas, if we are to believe MacKellar's account, Donald McEwen Beg pursued a more aggressive policy towards Clan Mackintosh.

Neither John Dow McEwen nor Donald McEwen Beg are included in Allan's Bond of Assurance. Indeed, John Dow does not appear in the records again after offering fealty ot the Earl of Argyll alongside his erstwhile enemy in 1577 (above). With the return of the young chief, his role as Tutor had come to an end. He is not included in Allan's Bond of Assurance because he needs no assurance of peace, and neither would it be appropriate for Allan to assert authority over his patron and benefactor. The family of Erracht had acted as Allan's tutors, and were apparently still regarded favourably by his future father-in-law even after the death of Donald Dow McConnell.[97] There is no evidence to suggest they ever opposed Allan's return, and every reason to imagine that John Dow McEwen supported him wholeheartedly.

Balhaldie claimed that 'the tutor', whom he supposed to be John Dow McEwen of Kinlochiel, 'was seized and beheaded at Dunstaffnage' at the instigation of the Earl of Argyll,[98] and Ardvorlich is adamant that, according to Dunstaffnage tradition, John Cameron of Kinlochiel was executed at Dunstaffnage Castle in 1585.[99] Since John Dow McEwen of Kinlochiel was apparently killed in 1550, this tradition (if it has any truth to it) may refer either to the real tutor, John Dow McEwen of Erracht, or perhaps to John McAne Dow of Kinlochiel.[100]

The later career of Donald McEwen Beg

The return of the young chief Allan McConnell Dow of Lochiel to Lochaber in 1578 will have been welcomed by his supporters in Erracht and may have attracted some of the breakaway elements in his clan to return to the fold,[101] but while a rival claimant to the chiefship remained in Donald McEwen Beg in Mamore, there could be no miraculous reunification of the divided clan. In 1582, a bond by 'Donald Makewin Vikconill in Manmoir'[102] records an agreement with Lachlan Mackintosh and others by which, 'the said Lauchlan has set to him and his subtenants the half of the lands of Glenloy and Locharkik with their pertinents in the country of Lochquhabir, and has given to him the service and manrent of the tenants of the other half;' the Earl of Argyll and James Campbell of Ardkinglass appear as cautioners.

Exactly how this treaty came about is something of a mystery, but it must indicate that the vendetta which Donald McEwen Beg is said to have pursued against Clan Mackintosh had come to an end. Thirteen years before, Donald McEwen Beg had apparently villified Donald and John Dow McEwen for coming to terms over the Disputed Lands, but now he had done the same himself. In the period of peace which ensued, the divisions which had once split the clan must have seemed increasingly insignificant.

This agreement seems to have come to an end in 1598, when the same lands were half wadset and half let to Allan McConnell Dow Cameron of Lochiel for nineteen years[103] and, in the same year, another paper records the gift of a fine cloak to Donald McEwen Beg by Lachlan Mackintosh of Dunachton, presumably as recompense for the termination of their earlier agreement.[104] Our usual image of Donald McEwen Beg is conditioned by MacKellar's presentation of him as *an Taillear Dubh na Tuaighe*, 'the Black Tailor of the Axe', a hard-bitten warrior with a visceral loathing of Clan Mackintosh, but these contemporary documents reveal that Donald could deal as effectively in the arts of peace as the arts of war. By their agreements with Lachlan Mackintosh, both Donald McEwen Beg and Allan McConnell Dow acknowledged Mackintosh suzerainty over the Disputed Lands, just as the McEwens of Erracht had done in 1569.

When Donald McEwen Beg finally left Lochaber, it was apparently unexpected, and his disappearance would remain a subject of interest in Lochaber even after 300 years. In 1883, MacKellar recorded that he had last been seen after a battle against Clan Mackintosh at Mucomir near Gairlochy, climbing the slopes of Beinn Bhan by the stream Allt Coire Choille-rais; MacKellar wrote that he 'was never seen in Lochaber again'.[105] According to both traditional accounts, Donald McEwen Beg disappeared so completely from Lochaber that he was believed to have been killed by Allan

McConnell Dow of Lochiel. Indeed, from Balhaldie's account, we might guess that Allan himself helped foster this story.[106] However, we know today that this story was pure invention. Reliable oral traditions of the Taylor family of Cowal confirm that they are descended from Donald McEwen Beg, *an Taillear Dubh*, who settled on Cowal near to Strath Eck (Gaelic, *Strath Eachaig*).[107]

Although Donald McEwen Beg may have lived out his days at Strath Eck, after 1598 he disappears from the historical record. In Lochaber, his later life was either unknown or forgotten. His descendants in Argyll abandoned the Cameron name and were known by the surname Taylor. After an astonishing career in the midst of his clan, Donald retired to a life of relative obscurity.

The early chiefship of Allan McConnell Dow XVI of Lochiel

A Commission under the Quarter Seal of 16 May 1588 lists men of Clan Cameron as brigands, who 'daily and nightly go abroad in bands, oppressing and sorning on the lieges, committing murders, thefts and other crimes'. This document names sons of both Donald Dow and John Dow McEwen of Erracht immediately after 'Allan McConill Dow, captain of Clanchamron', who heads the list.[108] Alongside them were the sons of Ewen McAne who had witnessed Allan's Bond of Assurance in 1578, followed by the sons of Allan McEwen who had appeared on both sides of the feud in the Contract of Mutual Defense in 1570. But significantly, there are no MacMartins of Letterfinlay and no MacSorleys of Glennevis in this list, and at this date these families probably remained loyal to Donald McEwen Beg.

Erracht men appear again beside 'Allane Camroun of Locheldy' in the Moyness Raid of 1598, where 'Johnne Badach McVcEwene of Errach, [and] his brother Ewne' (sons of John Dow McEwen) are named with their chief as participants in just the sort of crime which had been described in the Commission under the Quarter Seal ten years before, and the raiders are vividly described as 'all bodin in feir of weir, with bowis, darlochis, and tua handit swordis, steilbonnettis, haberschonis, hacquebutis and pistolettis'.[109] This time however, the list also includes 'Allaster McAllaster of Glenneves' and three MacMartins led by 'Duncane McMertine of Letterfindlay'. Thus, as soon as the agreement over the Disputed Lands between Lachlan Mackintosh and Donald McEwen Beg came to an end, Camerons of all stripes joined forces under their new chief Allan McConnell Dow of Lochiel for a symbolic first foray.

However, internal divisions would once more disturb the clan in the years 1612-3. These divisions were apparently fostered by a territorial dispute between the Earl of Argyll and the Marquess of Huntly, and do not appear to be connected with the previous dispute. Indeed, according to the Clerk of the Privy Council, Huntly found that 'Allane and his frendis stoode in termes of love and friendschip', and so he resolved to 'mak some dissensioun amangis thame', by offering all of Lochiel's lands 'to the speciallis of his friendis'. Faced with such temptation, the leading men of the clan succumbed to self-interest and sought to gain at their chief's expense, but the new fault lines were somewhat different from those of forty years before.

Land ownership seems not have been the only issue which divided the clan at this time. In 1612, Allan McConnell Dow denounced 'John [Bodach] Camroun McVcEwne in Errache, Ewne Camroun, his brother, Johnne McDonald Camroun, his brother's son' and others for refusing to support him in his commission against Clan Gregor, because they were 'loath that ony suche course tak effect in thair personis, bot that rather the saidis Allane and Allaster McDonald sould have followit the wicked and unhappie trade of the rebellious lymmairis of the Heylandis and Illis ... undir thair patrocinie and protectioun…'[110] Although Donald Dow McEwen of Erracht had once led Clan Cameron against the MacGregors, the political situation had changed dramatically since the 1560's when Campbells and MacDonalds had worked together as allies. Allan's continuation of this old policy now set the Camerons at odds with their former overlords and was deeply unpopular with the clan.

The situation was dramatically resolved when Allan McConnell Dow is said to have slain 20 of his kinsmen who stood as his opponents, teaching the survivors 'in quhat forme they sall carye thame selffis to their Chief heirefter'.[111] The *Register of the Privy Council* for 9 December 1613 names two of the men who were 'barbarouslie murdreist and slayne' by Allan as 'Johnne Camroun alias Bodache' the son of John Dow McEwen of Erracht, and 'Allaster Camroun of Glenneves' whose dispute in 1564 with Donald Dow McConnell XV may have been among the many factors leading up to the old chief's imprisonment in 1567. The same document also indicates that, as well as asserting his position through violence, Allan McConnell Dow had reversed his policy towards Clan Gregor to accommodate the loyalties of his wider clan.[112] Through these twin actions he demonstrated that, unlike his ill-fated father, he fully understood the nature of power in contemporary Scotland, and possessed the qualities necessary to maintain it. However, this brief episode had cost the lives of many more Cameron men than are known to have died in the whole ten years of the Erracht Feud.

Feud and justice in sixteenth-century Scotland

Feud was an inevitable feature of a society dominated by semi-autonomous kindreds or clans. Whilst to modern eyes, any feud may seem to constitute a breakdown of law and order, these conflicts were often played out according to a commonly recognised set of rules. Although universally understood, these rules were rarely explicitly articulated, but the contemporary legal measure of 'assythment' (compensation due to kinsfolk for death through feuding) implicitly recognises the feud as a regular function of society. Indeed, the right to take vengeance could even be enshrined in law and has been described by historian Jenny Wormald as 'a recurrent theme of medieval and early modern legislation'.[113] Thus, the entire narrative of the Erracht Feud was played out within an established quasi-legal framework. Rules governing the practice of feuding clearly went beyond written law into custom and tradition, and can only be properly understood by analysing the process of individual feuds such as this.

Although past commentators have tended to emphasise the violence of Highland feuding, the peaceful resolution of such disputes can be equally remarkable. Settlements could be brokered by social superiors like Argyll, who were somewhat removed from the immediate issues, but they relied on the commitment of the feuding parties to keep the peace for the future. Unlike Grey Colin's feud with Clan Gregor, the Erracht Feud was never prosecuted 'to the uttermost'. Despite the apparent division of the entire clan into feuding factions, violence within Clan Cameron remained minimal and was clearly directed towards specific and meaningful ends. After 1598, the entire clan accepted a single solution to the conflict; both factions put aside their differences as (perhaps under pressure from Huntly and Argyll) Donald McEwen Beg finally withdrew to allow unity and resolution.

Feuds were most common between separate clans but, as Keith M. Brown has shown in his analysis of the period of fifty years or so following the Erracht Feud, approximately one in every seven feuds was in fact between kinsmen of the same surname who would have shared the same clan identity.[114] The order and stability of traditional Highland society was based on bonds of kinship and 'fictive' kinship. The forces which governed interactions between the clans were the same as those which operated within an individual clan and, by the same token, the processes which led to inter-clan feuding can also be seen at work within the clan. Each clan kinship group was composed of smaller kinship groups, which were held together by common consent. If this consent was withdrawn a clan could split into factions,[115] and this is what happened in Clan Cameron during the minority of Allan McConnell Dow from 1567 to 1577, when the loyalties of the smaller kindred groups, cadet houses and 'septs' lay with alternative candidates for overall chiefship.

The Erracht-Lochiel Law-Suit of 1794

More than two centuries after John Dow McEwen of Erracht had withdrawn from Cameron politics in favour of Allan McConnell Dow of Lochiel, a dispute arose within the clan whereby a Cameron of Erracht did indeed attempt to claim the chiefship of the clan for himself.

In 1792, Allan Cameron of Erracht registered arms with Lyon Court as Chief of Clan Cameron, but his matriculation was rescinded in 1795, when Lyon Court declared that he had been only been accepted as the Representative of Clan Cameron 'in consequence of a misrepresentation of Facts' and that 'the said Patent [had] been obtained upon Misinformation and Misrepresentation . . . and Retained by the said Allan Cameron contrary to good Faith . . .'[116]

Perhaps even at this date, Allan Cameron of Erracht was already influenced by a misreading of the events of 1567-77 and believed he was reinstating a historical claim, but it is more likely that Allan opportunistically fabricated the Erracht claim from a standing start. Almost certainly, the law suit of 1794 has distorted modern understanding of the unrelated sixteenth-century feud. The Lochiel-Erracht case would have been relatively recent history for the historian Donald Gregory when he wrote his *History of the Western Highlands and Isles of Scotland*, as well as for the poet Mary MacKellar when she wrote her letter to *The Celtic Magazine*, and it undoubtedly conditioned their view of earlier Cameron history. This eighteenth-century legal battle has prejudiced opinion to the extent that even the standard work on Cameron history states that, 'the Camerons of Erracht, ever since 1550 or possibly before, had considered that they were the rightful chiefs of Clan Cameron.'[117]

In view of this later spurious claim, it is worth stating categorically that the Camerons of Erracht did not claim the chiefship in their own right during the sixteenth century and, whilst they were undoubtedly responsible for the death of Donald Dow McConnell XV in 1569, their other actions were consistent with their legitimate role as tutors for the chief Allan McConnell Dow of Lochiel XVI during his minority.

Conclusion

We are fortunate that there is a wide variety of evidence available to shed light on the progress and significance of the Erracht Feud. Traditional accounts of these events have preserved a sense of their drama which is easily overlooked when perusing the dry legal documents of the time, but they have also preserved the bias of contemporary agendas rooted in internal clan politics which, combined with the natural corruption to which such traditions are prone, has made them a distorting mirror. The two traditional accounts offer very different perspectives on the feud, but both are to some degree hostile to the Camerons of Erracht and, whilst this bias may be natural to these sources, in the absence of an equivalent tradition to tell the Erracht side of the story, our too-ready reliance on narrative traditions has helped distort our view of the original events, so that contemporary records have been read in the light of a preconceived opinion.

Although the basic plotline of Balhaldie's account of the Erracht Feud is substantially correct, it has led to the consistent misidentification of the leading antagonists. There does not appear to be any contemporary written evidence that either Ewen McEwen of Erracht or John Dow McEwen of Kinlochiel were ever involved in any rebellion against the chiefship of Lochiel. Indeed, it is almost certain that John Dow McEwen of Kinlochiel, who has traditionally been considered one of the principal authors of the feud, had in fact been dead for nearly 20 years before the quarrel began. There is no record for the death of Ewen McEwen of Erracht, but evidence suggests that he too was already dead before the start of the feud, and it was in fact his sons who took the lead role in the feud which has come to be called after their particular branch of the Cameron clan.

Although they were undoubtedly responsible for the death of Donald Dow McConnell XV, there is no evidence to suggest that Donald and John Dow McEwen tried to take control of the wider clan on their own behalf. Instead, it appears they acted in the name of the old chief's son Allan McConnell Dow, and although their rule as Tutors of Lochiel would be remembered by Balhaldie as a time of 'intolerable insolence and cruelty', there would seem to be no reason to believe that they were in any way disloyal to their young chief, Allan McConnell Dow of Lochiel XVI.

At the time of his death, Donald Dow McConnell's chiefship had already been rejected by the clan, and the authority of Erracht was accepted without question during the period of his imprisonment. However, the old chief's death clearly polarised opinion within the clan and roused the ire of John Grant of Freuchie, whose kinsman Donald McEwen Beg became the focus for opposition not only to the Tutors of Lochiel but also, by implication, to Lochiel himself. In 1578, when Allan returned to Lochaber to take up the chiefship in his own right, these divisions were not immediately resolved, and his cousin Donald McEwen Beg would continue to wield influence as an independent power within the clan for another twenty years.

Thus, despite its generally accepted name, the Erracht Feud of the late sixteenth century was in reality a standoff between the allied families of Erracht and Lochiel on the one hand, and Donald McEwen Beg on the other.

Notes

1. The broad outlines of Cameron history may be read in various books. The standard reference is by John Stewart of Ardvorlich, *The Camerons: A history of Clan Cameron* (Glasgow, 1974 (1981)).
2. Patronymics were commonly used to distinguish family members, who all shared the same clan name and often drew on a very limited number of personal names. Such patronymics are used consistently in contemporary documents cited in this study. Most are completely self-explanatory, but note that 'McAne' indicates 'son of John', and 'McConnell' is the usual form of 'McDonald', 'son of Donald'. In this book for the sake of clarity, I have used the prefix 'Mc-' to denote a patronymic, while 'Mac-' denotes the name of a clan or sept.
3. Stewart of Ardvorlich, 27.
4. Adam & Learney, *Clans Septs and Regiments*, 110, 172; Newton, *Warriors of the Word*, 131.
5. It's possible that the old chief had always intended the chiefship to descend through the senior branch of his descendants, and that he had already appointed Ewen Beg McConnell as tanist before his death. One motivation might have been political, since the mother of Ewen McEwen of Erracht was the sister of the Mackintosh chief who was responsible for Ewen McAllan's death. Nonetheless, this could be interpreted as a shift towards inheritance through primogeniture and away from tanistry.
6. *The Memoirs of Sir Ewen Cameron of Lochiel* are discussed more fully below, p11-12; cf. Appendix I i.
7. William Crawfurd & Robert Pitcairn (eds.), *Memoirs of Sir Ewen Cameron of Lochiell, Chief of the Clan Cameron*, 33-4; Appendix I i
8. David MacGibbon & Thomas Ross, *The Castellated and Domestic Architecture of Scotland from the twelfth to the eighteenth centuries)*, III, 87-90.
9. Mary MacKellar located the site of Ewen Beg's imprisonment at 'Inch-Connel Castle, in Eilean-na-Cloiche, Lochow', which would appear to confuse the island of Innis Chonnell in Loch Awe with that of Eilean na Cloiche in Loch Linnhe. There is no castle at Eilean na Cloiche, and there seems no reason to believe that MacKellar's tradition was reliable on this point (MacKellar's letter, 269; Appendix I ii).
10. The tradition that this Allan was actually the son of Donald Dow McConnell's brother, John Dow is discussed below.
11. Mary MacKellar, 'To the Editor of The Celtic Magazine', *The Celtic Magazine* 8 (1883), 268-74; Appendix I ii.
12. Alexander Mackenzie, *History of the Camerons*, 46-63.
13. MacKellar's letter, 269; Appendix I ii; cf Adam & Learney, 120.

14 'Allaster McEnduy Camroun' and 'Donald McEn[duy] Vic Donnald Camroun' who appear in Privy Council records for 1612 may be early representatives of this *Sliochd Iain Duibh* (J H Burton & D Masson (eds.) *Register of the Privy Council of Scotland, 1st Series*, IX 337).
15 John Dow McEwen of Kinlochiel was the son Ewen McAllan XIII, and was thus the brother of Donald McEwen (father of Donald Dow McConnell XV) rather than his son.
16 J Beveridge & G Donaldson (eds.) *Register of the Privy Seal of Scotland*, vi, 198; see below. Although MacKellar claimed that contemporary documents regularly refer to the XVIth chief as Allan McAne rather than Allan McConnell, this does not appear to be the case.
17 Dr Charles Fraser-Mackintosh, 'Minor Highland Septs - No. IV The Camerons of Letterfinlay, styled "Macmartin"', *TGSI*, 31.
18 Donald Gregory, *History of the Western Highlands & Isles of Scotland, 1493-1625*, 229.
19 Thus for instance, Gregory wrote of Donald McConnell's murder that 'the chief instruments of his death seem to have been his uncles, Ewin, founder of the house of Erracht and John, founder of that of Kinlochiel, younger sons of Ewin Allanson' (Gregory, 202-3). More recently Ardvorlich has followed suit, noting that, 'Gregory, Mackenzie, and Balhaldie, all state that there were two tutors for young Allan ...; Ewen of Erracht and John of Kinlochiel', although he also notes that it would appear to have been Ewen's son Donald who was assassinated in 1570 (Stewart of Ardvorlich, 273).
20 Robert Pitcairn, *Ancient Criminal Trials in Scotland*, I, i 355; Stewart of Ardvorlich, 276. The dead man's identity seems to be confirmed by the fact that his cousin John Stewart of Strathgarry was killed alongside him (Stewart of Ardvorlich, 272).
21 *Memoirs of Sir Ewen Cameron*, 34-6; Appendix I i.
22 Stewart of Ardvorlich, 276-7; the charter under the Great Seal is known from Balhaldie's manuscript *Inventorie of the Charters, etc. of the Family of Cameron of Locheile* (1727) where it is erroneously dated 6th March 1567; Ardvorlich suggests this should read 1563.
23 Stewart of Ardvorlich, 177.
24 Donald's grandfather Ewen McAllan XIII had held these lands from the Crown, but they had been attainted before his execution in 1546.
25 *Privy Council of Scotland*, I 291, 293, 294-5.
26 GD112/39/5/21; *Campbell Letters* 52.
27 GD112/39/3/12; *Cambell Letters* 78; Appendix I iii.
28 GD112/39/6/2; *Campbell Letters* 79.
29 According to a letter from William Stewart of Grandtully, 'clane Ewyn WcEwyn' had contacted the Earl of Atholl to enquire on behalf of their clansmen (GD112/39/12/8; *Campbell Letters*, No.81; Appendix I iv). Later tradition assigns the Gaelic name *Sliochd Eoghain mhic Eoghain* to the Camerons of Erracht (Adam & Learney, 540).

30 The use of the word 'clan' in this letter is paralleled by similar references to the Cameron families of Clan Alan VcAne and Clan Innes VcAne in Alan McConnell Dow's Assurance of 1577 (Appendix I xix), and does not in itself suggest an autonomous kindred separate from the rest of the clan.
31 GD112/39/4/23; *Campbell Letters* 51.
32 An incomplete charter for the grant of the same lands to Lachlan Mackintosh still exists in the National Archive, dated '156-' (NAS GD176/84), indicating that the queen probably always intended to regrant the lands to him as heir to William Mackintosh but had reason to delay.
33 NAS GD176/87; Appendix I v.
34 For a detailed consideration of Bonds of Manrent in this period, see Jenny Wormald, *Lords and Men in Scotland: Bonds of Manrent, 1442-1603* (Edinburgh, 1985).
35 Cathcart, *Kinship and Clientage: Highland Clanship 1451-1609*, 60-9, 75-7; Newton, 135.
36 *Memoirs of Sir Ewen Cameron*, 34; Appendix I i.
37 If Donald's father, Ewen McEwen Cameron of Erracht, had been alive (as according to Donald Gregory's interpretation of events) it should have been his name that appeared on this bond instead of his son Donald's.
38 An entry in the Register of the Privy Seal (*Privy Seal of Scotland*, No.1067, 198; Appendix I vii) gives wardship of 'the £20 land of Locheld, the 10 merk land of Lettir-Finlay, Stronabaa and Lindallie, and the £20 land of Niknodort in the Lordship of Lochquhaber' to John Caddell of Aslowne in the light of 'the decease of Donald Dow McConnell McKene or Camrum in 1569' and names the heir as 'Alan Dow McConell Makkene or Camrun, son of the said Donald'.
39 see for instance Stewart of Ardvorlich, 273.
40 "Report upon the state of Scotland in the reign of Queen Mary, written in A.D. 1594, and sent to Pope Clement the Eighth by the Jesuit priests in Scotland." translated from the early Latin copy among the Barberini MSS. by Joseph Stevenson (p.60).
41 GD112/39/12/15; *Campbell Letters*, No. 130; Appendix I xii.
42 *Memoirs of Sir Ewen Cameron*, 37; Appendix I i.
43 Alexander Nicolson, 1881, *A Collection of Gaelic Proverbs and familiar Phrases*, 368; Newton, 151.
44 James Toshach Clark (ed.) *Genealogical Collections concerning Families in Scotland, made by Walter MacFarlane 1750-51*; Appendix I vi.
45 Stewart of Ardvorlich, 2, 6, 8, 13, 14.
46 Mackenzie 1884, 14-16; Stewart of Ardvorlich, 8, 170.
47 Mackenzie 1884, 3, 28.
48 *Reg. Mag. Sig.* 9 January 1527-8; Mackenzie 1884, 41; Stewart of Ardvorlich, 23, 27, 33, 265.
49 NAS GD176/85; Lachlan Mor Mackintosh had been granted these lands as heir to his predecessor William Mackintosh XIII, who had been the uncle of Ewen McEwen of Erracht.

50　*Memoirs of Sir Ewen Cameron*, 37; Appendix I i.
51　J. R. N. MacPhail, 1896, 'Letters written by Mrs. Grant of Laggan concerning Highland affairs and persons connected with the Stuart cause in the eighteenth century' in *Wariston's Diary and other Papers*, SHS Vol. XXVI, 306.
52　Mackenzie 1964, xxii; Newton, 135, 145.
53　NAS GD176/187; MacFarlane, 260.
54　*Memoirs of Sir Ewen Cameron*, 188-193; Stewart of Ardvorlich, 72-3; Appendix I i.
55　Sir William Fraser, 1883, *The Chiefs of Grant*, III 141-2, No.138; Stewart of Ardvorlich, 279 No.14; Appendix I viii.
56　*Memoirs of Sir Ewen Cameron*, 37; Appendix I i.
57　Martin Martin, 1703, 1716, *A Description of the Western Islands of Scotland*, 109; Newton, 141.
58　Donald Meek, 1978, *The Campbell Collection of Gaelic Proverbs and proverbial Sayings*, No.642; Newton, 141.
59　Stewart of Ardvorlich, 274.
60　Donald McAllan is in Mamore on land belonging to the MacSorlies of Glennevis, whose predicament in 1564 may have helped build support for a coup by the Camerons of Erracht.
61　NAS GD176/129; Appendix I xx.
62　The two most prominent men listed among the 'latter parties', John McAllan of Callart and Martin McConaghy of Letterfinlay, will later be named among the assassins of Donald Dow McEwen of Erracht (NAS GD176/102; Appendix I xv).
63　GD112/39/12/15; *Campbell Letters*, No.130; Appendix I xii.
64　Newton, 151.
65　Newton, 134.
66　GD112/39/7/10; *Campbell Letters*, No.98.
67　GD112/39/7/21; *Campbell Letters*, No. 110; Appendix I ix.
68　GD112/39/8/4; *Campbell Letters*, No.112; Appendix I x.
69　GD112/39/8/4; *Campbell Letters*, No.112; Appendix I x.
70　GD112/39/8/6; *Campbell Letters*, No.114.
71　GD112/43/2/3; cf. *Campbell Letters*, p165 n3 (to No.112).
72　GD50/187/1; quoted by MacGregor 1989, 380.
73　GD112/39/8/19; *Campbell Letters* No.123.
74　GD112/39/12/12; *Campbell Letters*, No.106.
75　Glenorchy's apparent lack of concern may be partly because this incident was immediately overshadowed by a 'mischance' in which his own followers mistook Atholl's men for MacGregors, setting on them and killing them as they slept.
76　GD112/39/9/2; *Campbell Letters*, No. 127; Appendix I xi. Professor Jane Dawson's edition supplies the date from a nineteenth-century copy in the National Archives of Scotland (NAS GD50/116/64-5). Although the author of this letter and GD112/39/12/15 (*Campbell Letters*, 130) is identified in the editor's notes as Donald McEwen Beg, this

cannot be correct and she supports my re-identification of the author as Donald Dow McEwen of Erracht. The writer of these letters gives his name as 'Donald MacEvyn WicEvin in Lochaber' (NAS GD112/39/9/2; *Campbell Letters*, No. 127; Appendix I xi), and as 'Donald MacEvyn VicEvyn in Lochaber' (NAS GD112/39/12/15; *Campbell Letters*, No. 130; Appendix I xii). As the son of Ewen Beg McConnell, Donald McEwen Beg would have styled himself 'Donald McEwen VcConnell' (or 'VcDonnell') after his father Ewen Beg and his grandfather Donald Cameron.

77 GD112/39/12/15; *Campbell Letters*, 130; Appendix I xii.
78 GD112/39/9/10; Appendix I xiii.
79 GD112/39/11/10; *Campbell Letters*, No.180; Appendix I xiv.
80 NAS GD176/102; Appendix I xv.
81 This names on this list give some sense of who made up the faction opposed to Erracht; other names may be added from the Contract of Mutual Defence of 1570, and from the Assurance by Allan McConnell Dow of 1578. Ewen McAne and his brother Allan McAne were the sons of John McAllan, younger brother of the XIIIth chief, Ewen McAllan Cameron of Lochiel. Several names are repeated between these sources: Clan VcAllan VcAne appears in one form or another in all three documents and, where 'Angus McAne Vc[Mer]tene' appears in the Letter of Gift, Clan Innes VcAne VcMartin appears in the Assurance.
82 *Memoirs of Sir Ewen Cameron*, 38; Appendix I i.
83 J H Burton & D Masson (eds.) *Register of the Privy Council of Scotland, 1st Series*, II, 587-8, 589; Appendix I xvii; cf. Alasdair Campbell of Airds 2002, *A History of Clan Campbell: From Flodden to Restoration* (Vol.II), 81. The Privy Council scribe has apparently confused the Gaelic names Eoin and Eoghain, so that they mistakenly appear as sons of an Allan McEwen, but their uncle's name, 'Ewin McAne, Capitane of Inverlochy, their fader brother', is given correctly. This incident probably reveals more about relations between Atholl and Argyll than about Clan Cameron
84 *Privy Seal of Scotland*, No.1067, 198; Appendix I vii.
85 *Justiciary Court Book* (Old Series) Vol. XIII; Pitcairn, *Criminal Trials*, I, ii 33; Appendix I xvi. Just as the Letter of Gift reveals the supporters of Donald McEwen Beg, so this document gives us the names of some of the principals of the Erracht faction.
86 Stewart of Ardvorlich, 272, 278.
87 GD112/39/12/15; *Campbell Letters* No.130; Appendix I xii.
88 Campbell of Airds, 82.
89 *Argyll Transcripts VII*, 27; Appendix I xviii.
90 Donald Dow McEwen's reliance on Glenorchy in particular is apparent from his letters, and Donald McEwen Beg's with Argyll through is mentioned by Balhaldie, 38; Appendix I i.
91 Balhaldie names him as Lachlan Maclean; Appendix I i.
92 *Memoirs of Sir Ewen Cameron*, 37; Appendix I i.

93 *Maith an Chairt Ceannas na nGaoidheal*, Bateman's translation; Bateman & MacLeod 2007, *Duanaire na Sracaire*, 152-3. This poem may have been composed for Archibald Campbell, 5th Earl of Argyll (d.1573). A similar sentiment is expressed in a poem from as early as the 1520's, *An Duanag Ullamh* addressed to Colin Malach, 3rd Earl of Argyll (another version of this poem was composed for Colin's son, Archibald or Gillespie Roy, the fourth earl) while a third poem, *Dual ollamh do thriall le toisg*, which may date from about 1595, addresses the 7th Earl as *rí (na n)Gaoidheal*, 'king of the Gaels', and as *iarla Gaoidheal*, 'earl of the Gaels'. ll 48, 120 and ll 129, 14; quoted by McLeod 2013 'Caimbeul Poetry of the Sixteenth Century', 244.

94 NAS GD176/74; Appendix I xix.

95 The list of Camerons receiving Allan's assurance is broadly similar to the list named in the Contract of 1570. It may be somewhat surprising to find the sons of Ewen McAne among the witnesses to this charter, but if we are to judge from Balhaldie's narrative, Allan was faced with competing versions of the events of the previous ten years. More than any part they had played in past events, what mattered was their future loyalty to Allan as the new chief. There could be no other way to restore unity to the divided clan.

96 The sons of John Dow McEwen of Erracht referred to here are John Bodach and Ewen who, in contemporary documents, are given the designation 'McVcEwen' rather than the expected patronymic McAne (*Privy Council of Scotland*, V 498-9, IX 337)—this usage reflects the terms 'clane Ewyn WcEwyn' and 'Clan Ewin WikEwin' seen in the Campbell letters (NAS GD112/39/12/8, GD112/39/7/21; *Campbell Letters*, Nos. 81, 110; Appendix I iv, ix), and the Gaelic term *Sliochd Eoghain mhic Eoghain* (Adam & Learney, 540), and signifies that the Erracht family was already regarded as a distinct cadet branch or *sliochd*. The eighteenth-century armiger William Macewan of Glenboig (ob.1813), whose coat of arms is replete with Cameron symbolism, may have been descended from these McVcEwens of Erracht (*Lyon Register* 1, 573; Ewing, John Thor (ed.) 2016 *Clan Ewen, Some Records of its History: A new facsimile edition*, 44, Fig.3).

97 John Stewart of Appin's intervention on their behalf indicated in Atholl's letter of 28 June 1570 is noted above: GD112/39/7/21; *Campbell Letters*, No. 110; Appendix I ix.

98 Memoirs of Sir Ewen Cameron, 38; Appendix I i.

99 Stewart of Ardvorlich, 40, 211, 275, 276 n.13.

100 A 'John McAne Dwe McEwyne of Kandlochele' (presumably the son of John Dow McEwen of Kinlochiel slain in 1550) is named as a fugitive from justice in 1588 (Edinburgh, National Archives of Scotland NAS GD176/150), so a connection between Kinlochiel and the man executed at Dunstaffnage in 1585 seems unlikely, although it remains possible either that the date of execution is an error for 1588, or that John McAne of Kinlocheil had already been apprehended and executed when he was named in 1588 among a long list of miscreants still thought to be at large by the authorities in Edinburgh.

101 The sons of Ewen McAne, who had previously been arraigned for their part in the killing of Donald Dow McEwen, are named as witnesses in Allan's Bond (NAS GD176/74; Appendix I xix).
102 NAS GD176/129; Appendix I xx.
103 NAS GD176/187; Appendix I xxii; cf. MacFarlane, 260.
104 NAS GD176/185; Appendix I xxi.
105 MacKellar's letter, 272-3; Appendix I ii.
106 *Memoirs of Sir Ewen Cameron*, 38; Appendix I i.
107 MacKellar's letter, 273-4; Appendix I ii.
108 NAS GD176/150.
109 Complaint by John Dunbar of Moyness, George Dunbar in Clune and William Falconer in Lethinbar, *Privy Council of Scotland*, V 498-9.
110 *Privy Council of Scotland*, IX 337.
111 *Privy Council of Scotland*, X 818-20.
112 *Privy Council of Scotland*, X 185-9 and XI 337.
113 Wormald 'Bloodfeud, Kindred and Government', 65, cf. more generally 62-5.
114 Keith M Brown, *Bloodfeud in Scotland*, 76.
115 Wormald 'Bloodfeud, Kindred and Government', 66-9.
116 *Lyon Register I*, 567; Stewart of Ardvorlich, 303
117 Stewart of Ardvorlich, 298
118 Plutarch, *Moralia*, transl. W. W. Goodwin. A Latin translation of the text was published by Erasmus as *Apophthegmatum opus* in 1540, and he cited the story as an example of a 'wordless symbol' in his *Lingua* of 1525. An English translation by Nicolas Udall, *The Apophthegmes of Erasmus*, was published in 1564.
119 *Dictionary of National Biography*, VIII

Appendix I

Key sources and abstracts of sources for the Erracht Feud

i. From *Memoirs of Sir Ewen Cameron of Lochiel*, John Drummond of Balhaldie, 1737:

He [Allan McConnell Dow XVI] was, from his cradle to his grave, involved in a continued laberynth of troubles, which proceeded origionaly from the ill conduct and ambition of his tutors, whose views were suspected to extend furder than the simple administration of his affairs, which was all they could pretend to by their office. These were Donald and John Camerons, two of the younger sones of the famous Ewen McAllan, grand-uncles to the minor, and the predecessors of the Familys of Errocht and Kenlochiell, now considerable tribes of that clan. In a word, the conduct of these gentlemen were such, that Locheil's nurse, for the safety of his person, conveyed him privatly to Mull, where he remained during his infancey ...

Though the safety of the young Chief was thus secured, the conduct of the tutors keept all in confusion att home, for they acted more like proprietors than administrators. The rents and revenues of the estate, which was very large, they applyed to their own use, and having formed a faction among the Camerons, whom they corrupted by bribs and offices to an absolute dependence on their intrest, they lorded it over the rest of the Clan with intolerable insolence and cruelty. To make head against them, the opposite faction called home Donald McEwan, the bastard sone of him that was killed in the Isle of Lochow. He ... had the reputation of a youth of good sense and spirit.

His arrivall in Lochaber occasioned a kind of civil war, whereof Lachlan, then Laird of Macintosh, taking advantage, marched into the country at the head of such a body of men, as the tutors, in their present situation, were unable to resist, and obliged them to submitt to a treaty whereby the estate in dispute was sett to them on lase for a certain number of years, for the yearly payment of 80 merks Scots, an inconsiderable rent. But such, however, as gave Macintosh all the right and title to the estate that they could bestow, or be demanded during the minority of the Chief.

The tutors were sensible enough of the false step they had made, but as necessity had forced them into it, so they resolved to repudiat the contract, by a new invasion into the enemy's countrey, and in order to unite the Clan, they agreed to submitt all differances to the mediation of friends; this brought about a meeting of the partys att the old Castle of Inverlochy, where Donald the elder brother was barbarously murdered, by which their mutuall resentment and hatred was kindled into greater fury than before. To suppress the other tutor, Donald the bastard had recourse to his grandfather, the Laird of McDougall, who prevailed with the Earl of Argyle, Justice-General, to espouse the quarrell. In short, the tutor was seized and beheaded at Dunstaffnage, a very old building, and one of the seats of the antient Scots Kings, before the destruction of the Picts.

In the meantime Locheill, then a youth of about 17 years, being solicited by the heads of the opposite faction, returned to Lochaber, where he was so mannaged and imposed upon by their artifice and cunning, that he gave way to the death of the bastard, whom they accused not only as author of the murder of the tutors, but as guilty of more criminal designs of depriving himself of his life and fortune, upon pretence that he was no bastard, but the sone of a lawfull marriage.

Whatever trewth was in these suggestions, his death was generally resented. Locheill leaving the management of his affairs to some of his nearest relations, gave out that he was to return to his Governour att Dunune, but stopt by the way att Appine . . .

Choiseing to reside att Appine till matters were fully settled at home, he fell into a missfortune that very near coast him his life . . .

The newes of this and several other adventures made his Clan impatient to have him among them. All their divisions were now at an end, and their Chief was of sufficient age and capacity to mannage his own affairs, so that he was welcomed to Lochaber with universall joy.

Memoirs of Sir Ewen Cameron, 36-9

ii. From Mary MacKellar's letter to the editor of *The Celtic Magazine*:
. . . let me correct two mistakes in your last issue. You say at page 150 that Donald, son of Ewen Allanson, left two sons, both of whom succeeded respectively to the estate of Lochiel, after the death of their grandfather. Now, instead of two sons, Donald Mac Eoghain left three sons, the youngest being Ian Dubh, or, as he was commonly called, "Ian Dubh Dhruim-na-Saille," his grandfather having given him that place as a "gabhail" or "gavel."

Though Ian Dubh did not succeed to the chiefship, yet he is historically the most important of the three brothers, as his son Allan became chief of the clan in his boyhood, and was the progenitor of all the chiefs from that time to the present day. . .

TAILLEAR DUBH NA TUAIGHE 'CHUIR AN RUAIG AIR MAC-AN-TOISICH.

EOGHAIN BEAG MAC DHO'ILL 'IC EOGHAIN succeeded his grandfather as chief of the Clan Cameron. He never was married, unless, indeed, he was handfasted according to the custom of the time to the lady who was the mother of his son—his only child. The lady was the daughter of Macdougall of Lorne.

This happened when Ewen was very young, and the lady's father concealed his resentment until Ewen was chief. He then, on some plausible pretence, got him to visit him, when he imprisoned him in Inch-Connel Castle, in Eilean-na-Cloiche, Lochow. He was slain there by one MacArthur, whilst his clansmen, headed by his foster-father, Mac 'ic Mhartinn of Letterfinlay, were trying to effect his escape.

His son, "Donull Mac Eoghain Bhig," was in his father's charge from his infancy, and was sent secretly to a tailor's wife, in Blar-na'n-Cleireach, or Lundavra, to be nursed, from which circumstance came the name of "An Taillear Dubh," by which he was known all his life. We find him named Donald, probably for his grandfather, and tradition says that he was brought up by Maclachlan of Coiruanan, hereditary standard-bearer to Lochiel, who became his foster-father.

The boy grew up to be a brave and wise man, famous for his powers of sarcasm and ready wit, but more so for the skill with which he wielded his battle-axe, the great weapon of the warriors of Lochaber. From this distinguishing qualification came his sobriquet of "Taillear Dubh na Tuaighe," which has clung to him through the ages.

It is said that when John of Kinlochiel and Ewen of Earrachd murdered their chief, "Donull Dubh Mac Dho'ill 'ic Eoghain," they thought the chiefship and estate would fall into their own hands, but in this they were sorely disappointed, for the widow of the youngest of their three nephews gave birth to twin sons. The eldest was, of course, at once proclaimed chief, whilst the youngest, who was Tanaistear, fell heir to the "gavel" of Druim-na-Saille, and became the ancestor of the Camerons of that branch.

Tradition says that the mother of these twin boys was a Mackintosh, and that she hated the clan of her spouse with a great hatred.

As the mother of young Lochiel she went to live in one of the homes of the chief, "Eilean na'n Craobh," and it is there that we find "Donald," or rather "Taillear Dubh na Tuaighe," first appearing prominently in tradition.

The "Taillear" hated the Mackintoshes, and nothing pleased him better than to wield his axe against them on the battle-field.

He, in return, was hated by the Mackintoshes, especially by Ian Dubh's widow, and by John of Kinlocheil, and Ewen of Earrachd, the sons of the second wife of Ewen Allanson, Marjory Mackintosh, said by some historians to be daughter of Lachlan Badenoch, and not of Duncan Mackintosh, as is said in the Memoirs of Sir Ewen Cameron of Lochiel, quoted by you on this head.

On the first occasion in which the "Taillear Dubh" appears in tradition as a hero he must have been a young man. There had been a skirmish with the Mackintoshes, in which many of them were slain. The "Taillear" was the person deputed to carry the tidings to the lady at "Eilean na'n Craobh," a task which many a brave man would shrink from, knowing the strong nature and the Mackintosh proclivities of the lady. The "Taillear" went fearlessly, and walked straightway into her presence, battle-axe in hand. The lady cried out sternly, "Thig a nuas, a Thaillear, ach fag do thuagh shios" (Come in, tailor, but leave your axe without), to which the young warrior responded,

"Far am bi mi fhein bi' mo thuagh" (Where I will be my axe will be).

"Ciamar a chaidh an latha?" (How did the day go?) asked the lady.

"Oh!" cried the tailor, "gheibheadh tu bian cait air da pheighinn agus rogha is tagha air planc " (You could get a cat's skin for twopence, and pick and choice for a plack). On hearing this, the lady in a rage threw the infant heir into the fire, and in a moment the "tailor " lifted his battle-axe above her head, crying—"A bhean a rug an leanabh tog an leanabh " (Woman who gave birth to the child, lift the child) which she instantaneously did.

There was then a council held among the clan as to what was to be done with this unnatural mother, for it was not thought safe to leave their young chief in the hands of one who had proved so unworthy of her position.

They decided, therefore, to send the lady back to her own people, as she had forfeited all right to be considered a member of the Clan Cameron. The manner in which this resolution was carried out was as follows:—She was placed on horseback with her face to the animal's tail, and so driven within the boundary line of the Mackintosh domains ... The clan also resolved not to leave the infant chief to the guardianship of his granduncles of Kinlochiel and Earrachd. He was, therefore, sent to Mull, probably to the widow of his uncle, Donald Dubh, who was a lady of the Duart family. "Donull Mac Eoghain Bhig" or "Taillear Dubh na Tuaighe" went meantime to reside with his grandmother, Lady Grant of Grant, from which place he was in the course of time called by a party of his clan, that he might protect them from the oppression of Kinlochiel and Earrachd, who were acting in a most autocratic manner towards them.

The "Taillear" became again their leader in battle, and it is said that in every field in which he fought against the Mackintoshes he was victorious. So successful was he that the people began to suspect that he had a fairy origin, and that a special charm was upon him. He was not only famous for his use of the "axe," but was fleet-footed as the mountain deer, which stood him in good stead on one occasion. He was out hunting, and accidentally fell into the hands of the Mackintoshes. They were quite jubilant over his capture, and longing to see his blood shed.

"Had I fallen into your hands like this what would you do with me?" asked the Mackintosh of his captive.

"I would at least give you a chance for your life, and if you could get free I would let you," replied the "Taillear."

"Then I shall do so with you. You will not have to say you outstrip the Mackintosh in generosity," exclaimed the chief.

He then formed his men into a ring, with the "Taillear" in the centre, saying, "Men, present your arms, and if he rushes upon you it will but make an end of him the quicker."

The "Taillear" began to wield his battle-axe, as if trying to make an opening here and there, by which he could escape. He threatened to break the circle at different points, and at length his quick eye saw where the men were beginning to be off their guard, and, making a sudden dash, he sprang from what seemed the arms of death. He ran as fast as his fleet feet could carry him, pursued by his enraged enemies, the foremost among them being their chief. At last the "Taillear" came to a broad ditch which he leaped lightly, and got safe across. The Mackintosh leaped after him, but fell into the mire. The "Taillear Dubh" raised his axe above his head, and said to the floundering chief, "Dh'fhaodainn, ach cha dean mi." "I might, but I will not." The Mackintosh, pleased with the generosity of his foe, waved his men back from the pursuit, and the "Taillear" gave him his hand and pulled him out of the ditch.

The place where this happened is not far from the banks of the Caledonian Canal at Gairlochy. The spot where he made the leap is to this day called "Leum an Taillear," and the ditch, though now filled up, still bears the name of "Lochan Mhic-an-Toisich."

Mucomer was the scene of his last battle with the Mackintoshes, and on the evening of that day he was seen climbing the mountain side at Coilleros, where there runs a stream known as "Ault-gormshuil," called after the celebrated Lochaber witch of that name. The "Taillear Dubh" was never seen in Lochaber again. All sorts of surmises were made about his disappearance. Some said he was murdered by command of the young chief, Ailean Maclan Duibh, who had now returned home. The enemies of the "Taillear Dubh" had made the young lad believe that he wanted to be chief himself; that he was stealing the hearts of the people with that intention; and that he asserted his being the child of a lawful marriage, and therefore not illegitimate. It is said that the chief believed these tales, and consented to the death of his relative. When he, therefore, disappeared, there was great indignation among his friends, who believed him to have been murdered.

Those who believed in his fairy origin thought now that he had gone back to his people, having fulfilled the work given to him to do. Others said that, being tired of fighting, he had retired to some Monastery, and that he was seen in the district of Cowal.

So great a favourite was this brave and unselfish man among his people, that their indignation waxed so hot against their chief as to make him again leave the country. The clan believed that he had consented to the murder of their hero; therefore, he did not feel safe among them, and he retired to Appin until their fury would abate . . .

After the fate of this brave man had been enveloped in darkness for centuries it is now accounted for, and made clear; and it is proved that the "Taillear Dubh" did seek safety in Cowal, where he married and left a family . . . Without knowing that any tradition existed in Lochaber about their ancestor, the Taylors of Stratheachaig knew that he was named "Taillear Dubh na Tuaighe," that his real name was "Donald Dubh," and that he was the offspring of a chief of Lochiel . . .

The "Taillear Dubh" was in special danger from the families of Earrachd and Kinlochiel, as in defence of the absent chief he had been the cause of the death of these veteran relatives, who were playing into the hands of their kinsmen, the Mackintoshes. Ewen of Earrachd was murdered at Inverlochy, where the opposing parties of the clan met in council; John of Kinlochiel was beheaded at Dunstaffnage by order of the Earl of Argyll, whom the "Taillear Dubh" got to espouse the quarrel through the influence of his grandfather, Macdougall of Lorne. When "Allan Mac Ian Duibh" returned again to take the power into his own hands and reign, he came to understand that his relative, "Donull Mac Eoghain Bhig," alias "Taillear Dubh na Tuaighe," had always been his best friend. He heard of how he had saved him from his heartless mother, and had watched over his interests through all the years of his absence. Then he was sorry that he had blamed him wrongfully, and to make amends, as well as to please his offended clan, he paid the memory of the brave man the compliment of placing him in his coat of arms as supporter on either side, with his battle-axe held up conspicuously. There he remains still, and his name lives in the songs, proverbs, and traditions of his native land; and next, perhaps, to the great Sir Ewen, he is their ideal warrior and hero. His name awakens their pride and their affection; and as long as there is a Cameron in Lochaber, or Gaelic spoken, there the name of "Taillear Dubh na Tuaighe" will be remembered.

The Celtic Magazine, Vol.8, 1883 pp.268-74

iii. Donald Dow, captain of the Clanchamberon, to Colin Campbell of Glenurquhay, 1565-6

To ane rycht honorabill man and my speciale frend Collyne Campbell off Glenorquhay

Rycht honorable Sir I recommend me hartlie to you. Forasmekele as I am informit that ye art suir displesit at me marweling heirof becauis I knaw nocht in quhat punctis I have offendit yow in ony promeis at ewir I promest. Thairfoir I wald youw advertesit me in wret the cauis of your displesser that I ma amend the samin to my wtermest power. And gif your Mastership will nocht wret the cauis ye sall adverteis gif ye will have me passand quhair ewir ye treist me and I salbe reddy heirto as ye chearge. I have advertest freindis that thair we ane band betuix you and me of guid nychtborsschepe quhairthrow gif ye had ocht ado that I suld be reddy with all my mycht tow do yow guid service as I sall ewir do salang as ye vill accept the samin, ye supportand me in lik manner. The rest of my mynd wer langsum to wrett bot as ye adverteis me with the berar sall do in that effaris to quhome ye pleis gif credens in lesummes for I have scheawin him part of my mynd. Referring the rest to your answer and Jesu be your Mastershipis keiper. Of Lochaber be yours at power.

GD112/39/3/12; *Campbell Letters*, No.51.

iv. William Stewart of Grandtully to Colin Campbell of Glenorchy, March 1566:

... my Lord of Athollis ... hes biddyn me schaw yow that clane Ewyn WcEwyn hes send to hym to caus desyr the men quhilkis ye hef in handis and he sayis he man request. Bot Sir for your awyn weil quhiddyr my Lord request slycht or vtherwayis I wald thynk best sawand your wysdome that ye rather gef thaim meit or than releffit thame on guid [cautioun] quhill ye saw greter trubil pacefeit.

NAS GD112/39/12/8; Campbell Letters, 81.

v. Bond of Manrent, 26 December 1567:

Bond of Manrent by Martyne McDonquhie Vic Martyne (on being put to liberty) to Donald McEwin Vic Ewin, whom he promises to serve faithfully, the said Donald giving him his own lands to hold as freely as he held them of Donald Dow. If Donald Dow shall be given up or relaxed McEwin is to redeem the said lands from Donald Dow, and if that cannot be done, or if McEwin cannot give him other lands as good, then he shall be free to serve Donald Dow. McEwin is also to receive all the surname of the said Martyne in favour.

Mackintosh Muniments 87; NAS GD176/87

vi. Agreement over Glen Loy and Loch Arkaig, 1569:

In the year 1569, Mackintosh leased to Donald McEwan, alias Cameron, and John his brother, the lands of Glenlui and Locharkaig, for their service and submission, for the sum of 80 merks yearly, as is contained in the agreement.

MacFarlane's Genealogical Collections, 238.

vii. Privy Seal, Edinburgh 1570/1:
Gift to John Caddell of Aslowne of the ward of nonentry of the £20 land of Locheld, the 10 merk land of Lettir-Finlay, Stronabaa, and Lindallie, and the £20 land of Niknodort in the Lordship of Lochquhaber and Shire of Inverness; for terms from the decease of Donald Dow McConnell McKene or Camrum in 1569 until the entry of the heir; with the relief of the same and the marriage of Alan Dow McConell Makkene or Camrun, son of the said Donald, or of other heir succeeding.

Privy Seal of Scotland, No. 1067, 198.

viii. Contract between Donald McCallan McEwin and John McCallan McAne and others, 4th April 1570:
At Daochmolowak in Strathpeffir within the erldome of Ross, the fowrt day of Aprile, in the yeir of God ane thowsand fyve hundreth and saxte ten yeris, it is appointit, agreit and finalie endit betuix honorabill and discreit persons, Donald McCallan McEwin in Mammoir in Lochchabir on that ane part, and Jhone McCallan McAne in Lochchabir, Alexandir his bruder thair, Martein McConoche Ekmartein thair, Jhone Dow McAne Ekane thair, Johne McNeill Ekane Ekcorilla thair, on the uthir part, in forme and effect as eftir follows: That is to say, the saidis Jhone McCallan Ekane, Alexander his bruder, Martein McConoche Ekmartein, Jhone Dow McAne Ekane, Jhone McNeill Ekane Ekcorilla, with thair freindis, servandis, assisteris and parttakaris, sail fortife, mantein and defend the said Donald McCallan in all and haill his efferis, querelis, and actionis, as he has ado contrar all mortale, the authoritie being exceptit onlie; and in lyke maner, the said Donald with his freindis, servandis and assisteris and parttakaris sail fortife, mantein and defend the saidis Jhone McCallan McAne, Alexander his bruder, Martein McConoche, Jhone Dow and Jhone MacNeill, thair freindis, servandis, assisteris and parttakkaris contrar all mortale, the authoritie being exceptit; and sail tak anfald part with utheris contrar all

mortale, being exceptit that is exceptit, ay and quhill tha haiff ane lauchfull cheif, tutor or curator, quha sail haif the steir and guvernance of thair cuntray of Lochchabir, to the quhilk cheif, tutor or curator, tha are bayth contentit to obey: And for observyng, keping and fulfilling of bayth the partes, bayth the parteis ar swarne to stand ferme and stable in keping of the premissis. In witnes heirof the parteis hincinde has subscrivit this present writt with thair handis led at the pen be the notar onderwrittin, as eftir followis, day, yeir and place aboune writtin; befoir thir witnes, honorabill and discreit men, Rore McAlexander of Borrodill, Jhone Dingwell apperand of Kyldoin, Hector McAlexander, Johne Reowch McLachlan Ekcallan, James McCallan, Alexander Wrquhart, servandis to McKenze, with utheris divers.

Chiefs of Grant, Vol.III, No. 138, 141-2

ix. Extract from John, 4th earl of Atholl, Blair in Atholl, to the laird of Glenurquhaye, his cousin, 28 June 1570:

As for the purpoiss that Johane Steuart of the Appin hes schawin yowe concerning the Clan Ewin WikEwin I pray yow desyr him to trawell thairintill and to spur thame to that affect and gif thai do ony thing that is wirthe reward ye salbe juge thairintill. For my part I haif send to thaim my self quho gifis me guid wordis heiranentt I wat nocht quhat thai will do.

NAS GD112/39/7/21; Campbell Letters, No. 110.

x. John, 4th earl of Atholl, Blair in Atholl, to the laird of Glenurquhay, his cousin, 8 July 1570

To his rycht trest cussing the Lard of Glenurquhay

Rycht trest cussing efter my hartly commendatiouns. Ye sall onderstand that the Clanewin hes promussit now to fulfyll that quhilk lang abeffor that quilk thair condesioun was quilk is to persew the Clangregor to the wttermaist quhilk I thocht goud to mak yow adwerteisement. Yit thay feir that in

cuming throcht your boundis for this affek that your serwandis and the Erlls off Argyllis quha ar now put furthe sall do thaim harme. Thair for wald haiff your assurrance that thay may freily pass throcht your cuntray for doing off the caussis forsaid quhilkis I think ye can nocht refuis. Asalsua [sic] thinkis best that ye gat thaim onderstand be soum way frome yow that ye will be thair freind gyff thai keip thair promeiss towart the persewing off the Clangregor and that thay sall haiff fre passaige throw your cuntray they keipand thair condesioun. In the primyss giff ye think ony wayis this purpoiss no goud adversteiss me again wtherwayis send me the assurrance to ... [text illegible] ... forsaid. Sua nocht willing to troubill yow ony forder at this present. Committis yow to God. From Blare in Atholl this vii day of July be your ... [text illegible]
[postscript ommitted]

NAS GD112/39/8/4; Campbell Letters, No.112

xi. Donald McEvyn WicEvin, in Lochaber to Colin Campbell of Glenurquhay, 2 August 1570:
To the rycht honorable and my trayst frend Collin Campbell of Glenurquhay deliver this

Rycht honorable Sir efter my maiste humlie recommendatioun. I have resavit your wrett and quhair your Maister prayis me to contennew in the service that I have beginnyn and that it is my Lord of Atholis and my Lord of Argilis will that the samin be performit and that your Maister sall revard me and my bruther efferand to our service. As to that wil God I sall pas in hest to my Lord of Athoill and witt of his Lordshipis mynd towartis my effaris. And in the mid tyme will send my servand to your Maister with my writt desyring yow to commend me thair. Gif it be possible quhair will God I sal end the mater with him to the effect that his Lordship sall have honour and your Maister gret proffett. For in guid faycht I ending the samen with his Lordship and yow I will nocht desist

fra pershewing of the Clangregor quhill we end the mater betux ws in that mater that we sall nocht leiff of the play quhill the tane part sall have ane end. I gettand your Maisteris labouris in performing of my guid erandis at his Lordshipis hand and as I put no dowit bot ye ma do the samen. Thairfoir I pray yow that ye wrett incontinent to my Lord towartis my effaris that I ma knaw of your labouris or I pas thair. For ye knaw I ma nocht guidlie pershew the Clangregor to the rigour quhill the be sum ordour put betux me and thais of my kyn that ar with Evyn Beg Soune. The rest of my mynd wer to lang to wrett bot at meting will God we sall end the mater in that maner that it sall cum to your plesour. And so committis your Maister in the protectioun of God. Of Lochaber the secund off August be your assurit freind with power,
  Donald MacEvyn WicEvin in Lochaber

  NAS GD112/39/9/2; Campbell Letters, No. 127.

xii. Donald McEwyn Vic Evin in Lochaber, Rannocht, to Colin Campbell of Glenurquhay, 'Thursday' August 1570:
To the rycht honorable and his traist freind Collin Campbell of Glenurquhay deliver this.

  Rycht honorable Sir and traist frend efter my hertlie commendatiounes. Pleis your Master be remembrit wpoun my last wretting to yow and vil God I will contennew in furthfillin of the punctis heirof sua your Mastership vill do the lik in furthfillling of your part towartis me and my bruther. And now instant I have past to commonid my Lord quhair I wald your Mastership ver present gif it be possible for thair in presence of my Lord we mecht end the mater in that manner that it mecht be honour to my Lord and gret proffit to yow. For quhow schwne I enter ernestlie in your bessines I will nocht desist thair fra quhill the samin be endit to my power. I am informit the Lard of Grant beis in Blair to furthset my freindis materis in my contrar quhairfor I wald ye ver present that I mecht knaw of your labouris. Bot I heir thair is sum drynes instant betuix my Lord and yow quhilk I traist in God vill nocht contennew forthair. My Lord hes writin to me that he wes miscontent of the deid that my bruther did last bot the samin is contennewit as yett. And without ye cum your self I pray you send me your gud cunsall and mynd or gif ye have wrettin to my Lord as I wret to you in my effaris or quhat wes his ansuer. I vill send ane servand of my awyn to commoun you or I pas hame with my mynd. Reffering the rest to your ansuer and God kepe you. Off Rannoch this Turisday be your,

    Donald MacEvyn VicEvyn in Lochaber

                              NAS GD112/39/12/15; Campbell Letters, No. 130.

xiii. Extract from William Maitland of Lethington, Blair in Atholl, to the laird of Glenurquhay, 11 August 1570:
As towart ... Donald Dow quhilk ye writt of I sall nocht faill quhan he cum[mis] heir to my Lord to speik and do samekill for him at my Lord Athollis handis as I may for your caus. And I sall lat him knaw your mynd towart him and the solistatioun of me for his purpois.

                                        NAS GD112/39/9/10.

xiv. Extract from William Stewart of Grantullye, Dunketh, to the [lady] of Glenurquhay, 19 October 1570
As to wdyr writingis ye desyrit to Lochchabir men my Lord of Atholl wald writ nayne bot sayis gif MacRennald and Donald Dow be willyng to cum to the Lard lat ilk ane of thame send ane special man to his Lordship and he sal declare thame his guid mynd to the Lardis contentment.

                            GD112/39/11/10; Campbell Letters, No.180

xv. Letter of Gift, 15 April 1572:
Letter of Gift by King James the Sixth, with the consent of John, Earl of Mar, Regent, to Lachlan McIntosche of Dunnauchtane, and his heirs and assigneees, of the eschaet goods of Donald McEwin VcOnill, Ewin McAne, John Crwacht McEwne VcAne, Allan McEwin VcAne, John McAllane VcAne, Allester Dow McAllane VcAne, Ewin McMaistir Johnne, John Dow McVcFaill, Paul McVcFaill, John McAlester Rovy, Allester McAllane VcAne VcCoull, Doule Dow McKonquhy VcAne VcCoule, John Dow McGilvorrie VcCoule, Doule McCoule VcFersoun, Mulmorrie McConile Roy, John McEwin VcKennich, Angus McAne Vc[Mer]tene, Duncan McAnguse McAne VcMertene, Soirle McConill VcAllane, Mertene McConquhy, Soirle McConquhy, Ewin McAne Voir VcMertene, John McAne VcMertene, who are at the horn at the instance of John Dow McEwin in Lochquhabir, brother of the deceased Donald Dow McEwin, and his remanent kin and friends, for not finding caution to appear in the tolbooth of Leith, and answer for the slaughter of the said Donald; dated at Leith, 15th of April 1572.

Mackintosh Muniments 102; NAS GD176/102

xvi. From Justiciary Court Book, 9 July 1572:
Johnne Dow MacKewyne WicKewyn, Doule Oig MacCoule MacCondoquhy Roy in Bar, Ewyne MacWilliame MaCayne Dow in Auchinlytht, and above thirty others.

Hugh Lord Fraser of Lovete, and Lachlan McYntosche of Dunnachtie, are fined xl li. for each of these persons, for thair non-appearance, to vnderly the law, for art and part of the slaughter of vmqle Donald Dow MacCoule WicEwyn, Captain of Clanranald. The principle parties 'adjudgeit to the horne.'

Justiciary Court Book (Old Series), Vol. XIII; Pitcairn, Vol. I, ii, 33; Stewart of Ardvorlich, 277-8.

xvii. Privy Council, 1577:

Anent the supplication presentit to my Lord Regentis Grace and Lordis of Secreit Counsale be Allaster Dow McAllane McEwin of Camroun, and Johnne Cam his broder of surnawm, makand mention.—That quhair Johnne Erl of Atholl, his servandis and utheris of his name—of casuing, command, assistance and ratihabitatioun, be force and way of deid, certane monethis syne or thairby, tuke and apprehendit the saidis complenaris and put thame in suir firmance and captivitie in his place of the Blair of Atholl, be quhat power, commissioun or authoritie thay knaw not, quhairin thay are maist extremillie handillit and detenit continewalie sensyne,—and on na wayis will put and caus put thame to libertie furth of the said ward, swa that thay may pas and behaif thame selffis for doing of thair lefull effairis and bissines as oure Soverane Lordis fre liegis,—without he be compellit ... The saidis Allister Dow and Johnne Cam comperand be Ewin McAne capitane of Innerlochy—thair fader broder, with Maister Thomas Craig their procuratour; and the said John Erll of Atholl comperand be Maisteris Johnne Scharp and Alexander Mauchane his procuratouris, be quhome it wes allegeit that the saidis Allister Dow and Johnne Cam wer denunceit rebellis and put to the horne, remaning thairat the tyme of thair apprehensioun as thay do yit, and thairfoir sould not put thame to libertie; and forder, that thay had committit divers slauchteris, heirschippis and oppressionis upoun certane the said Erllis men, tenentis and servandis, and utheris oure Soverane Lordis liegis, and wer fugitives fra the law thairfoir; and thairfoir thay being takin and apprehendit as rebellis and fugitives within his boundis and jurisdictioun—he havand power and authoritie thairto—aucht not to be put to libertie as is desyrit bot justice execute upoun thame, conforme to thair demerittis and lawes of this realme; and to that effect offerit and wes content to bring and present thame befoir my Lord Regentis Grace and Lordis of Secreit Counsale, or before the Justice or his deputtis, upon sic day as thay wald appoint to be tryit as efferis.

Privy Council of Scotland, II, 587-8

[Mr. Andro Abercrumby servitor of Johnne Earl of Atholl presented in his master's name Allister Dow McAllane VcEwin Camroun and Johnne Cam his brother, and also produced letters raised by the brothers and other friends of the late Donald Dow McKewin, by which the said Allister and Johnne were denounced for the slaughter of the late Donald.]

Privy Council of Scotland, II, 597

xviii. Bond of Manrent, 11 June 1577:
Bond by Donald mcewne vcdonill and John makewne whereby they "Compromis Bindis and oblissis ws be ye faith and treuth in our bodeis that we and ilkane of ws sall Inter to Colane erll of ergile our plegis following, to wit: for me ye said donald, Allescander dow makallene vcane, and for me ye said Johne, Allane my sone, obsyrving of our Band of Service maid to ye said noble lord of ye dait At Downone ye tent day of Junij 1577 betuix ye day and daitt heiroff and ye 2b day of Junij instant, bot any forthair delay be this our speciall obligatioun subsomirt be ye notar underwritin, at our command at Downone ye ellevint day of Junii 1577." Before these witnesses Dougall Campbell of Auchnobrek, dowgall Mcdowgall of dounolleiz, Ane reverend fader in god Johne bischope of ye Ilis commendatar of ycomkill and Ardchattane, duncane Campbell of Ormadill, duncane Campbell of Dounetrone and Colene Campbell of Ottir, James Campbell of Ardkinglas and James makdonill grwannyche. "And attour Becaus ye said noble Lord hes promest fre ward to ye said plegis Induring thair ward and Remanyng as plegis wit his Lordschip, we bind and oblissis ws & Ilkane of ws faithfullie to be souertais and cautionaris for ye said plegis anent thair trew remanyng with ye said noble lord and his Keparis of Game but any Removing or getting away unto ye tyme of yair fredome." Donald McEwne Vcdonill and Johne dow mcewne vcewine campbronis wit our handis led on ye pen be ye notar Dowgall McArthor.
(Dorso "Clan Camerons bond giveing pledge to observe there manrent 1577.)

Argyll Papers, *Argyll Transcripts VII,* 27
by kind permission of the Duke of Argyll

xix. Assurance be McConil duy to Makintoishie, 1577 (30 January 1578):

Be it kenned to all men by those presents,—Me, Allane Cameron, chief and captain of Clan Cameron, bearing the burden of my kin of Clan Cameron, that depends on me, or takes my part, to have assured, and by these presents assures, Lachlan Makintosh of Dunachton, his kin, friends, servants, roumes, steadings, and possessions, their bodies, goods and gear, moveable and immoveable. Further and by these presents, assures Clan Allane wec Ayne, Clan Innes wec Ayne Wec Ayne Vec Mertyne, Donald Dow McDonill Wec Ayne Vec Mertyne, and John McAyne Vec Ewyn Roy, with the rest of Seoldonquhy Vec Soarle, their bodies, goods, and gear, friends and tenants, tenants and subtenants, rooms, staedings and possessions, corne, and with all the lands that they possessed and manured last within the bounds of Mamore and Lochaber, to be unhurt, unharmed, or molested in any way by me, my kin or friends foresaids, with all others that I may stop or let from the day and date hereof, and that they shall win their goods and gear, with their servants and tenants, upon their own towns, and manure the same as peaceably, without impediment, made to them by me or any that I may stop, during the survivance of the said assurance; 'provyding that I nor nane in my name requyre mete, drink, nor service of thame during the tyme of this assurance, as said is, except McAyne Vec Evin Roy;' guid talik man (?). I, the forenamed Allane, binds and obliges me that I shall hold 'Johanne Dow McEvyn sonnis in thair awne rowmis quhill Witsonday sua that the giff me mete and drink resonable as utheris in the cuntreth, and that I sall have the service of thair tennendis that dwellis apon the grund.' The same assurance to stand firm and stable upon fifteen days' premonition, to be made at Innerloquhy, gif it be the Erle of Huntlie's pleasure. Be this my assurance given, written, and subscribed by me, at Lochele, the penult of Januar, 1557, before these witnesses—John Vic Allisetr Duff, the sons of Ewyn McAyne, Charles McWilliam, with others diverse.

[signed] ALLANE CAMRONE, LARD off LOCHEILL

Mackintosh Muniments 74; NAS GD176/74

xx. Bond by Donald Makewin Vikconill in Manmoir, Holyrood House, 28 February 1581-2:
Narrating that Lauchlane Malcomtosche of Dwnnachtane, as principal, and Sir John Gordoun of Lochinver, Patrick Gordoun of Auchindowne, Walter Ogilvie of Finlatter, George Ogilvie of Dunlugus, Thomas Stewart of Gairntullie, knights, and William Gordoun of Schevis, as cautioners, on 29th October 1581, enacted themselves in the books of Privy Council that neither the said Lauchlan nor any of his kin and dependents would molest the tenants of the earldom of Moray; and that the said Lauchlan has set to him and his subtenants the half of the lands of Glenloy and Locharkik with their pertinents in the country of Lochquhabir, and has given to him the service and manrent of the tenants of the other half; therefore he obliges himself, taking burden for his servants and dependents and friends, and with him Colin, Earl of Argyle, and James Campbell of Arkinglass, as cautioners, to relieve and keep scatheless the said Lauchlan Malcomtosche and his cautioners of all breaches of the said cautionry by any of his tenants, dwellers upon these lands, and that for seven years from Whitsunday 1582; promising also to relieve his own cautioners.
Witnesses: James, Lord of Downe, James Keyth, John Oigstoun and Mr. Robert Flescher.
[signed] *Ergyll.*
Mackintosh Muniments 129; NAS GD176/129

xxi. Discharge by James Petrie, Elgin, 30th April 1598
Discharge by James Petrie, merchant burgess of Elgin, to Lachlan McIntosche of Dunnauchten, for all that he was due to him, except the price of a cloak given at his command to Donald McKewin, valued at £14, 5s.
Mackintosh Muniments 185; NAS GD176/185

xxii. Heads of Agreement, Lachlan McIntosche of Dunnachteine and Allan Cambrone of Locheill, Forrachine, 8 July 1598

Whereby McIntoische is to wadset to Cameron for 6000 merks half of the lands of Glenloy and Locharkik, suspending the reversion for nineteen years, and to grant the other half in feu, for service only, with his bond of maintenance to him and his friends; it being stipulated that if the said Lachlan shall summon the said Allan and his friends for his service, that he will send one son of his own, and one son of Angus Williamson or James Glass, as pledges for their safe return. The price stipulated is to be paid partly in cattle, for which McIntosche is to send his men eight days before Michaelmas to Lochaber, that they may select them at the value of £10 apiece. Half of the money is to be deferred for a short time, and as cautioners for its payment, Cameron names the Lairds of Glenurquhie, Vembis and Garintillie. Cameron is to give his bond of service to McIntoshe, the authority and the Earl of Huntly being excepted; and in case of variance between Huntly and McIntosche, the latter is to be preferred. Breach of his bond of service on the part of Cameron is to imply forfeiture of his lease, and the determination of the fact is remitted to the arbitration of James McIntosche of Gask and Angus Williamsone in Termeit on the part of the said Lachlan, and of James Grant of Ardneidlie and Patrick Grant of Rothemurchus on the part of Cameron, with John Grant of Freuquhie as oversman; and should McIntosche wrongfully invade Cameron or his friends, the penalty shall be that the lands now wadset shall only be redeemable on payment of 12,000 merks, and a further lease of nineteen years. Any sudden slaughters between the clans are not to be reckoned breaches, but to be referred to the arbitrators. If Cameron die without leaving a son, this agreement is not to expire while John Moir McAllane VcEine, Alester McAlester VcConell in Gleneves, John McAlester Eine in Clir Lachlan, Duncan McMairteine in Lytirfyndlay, Donald John Dou McEine son, or Allan his brother, or Dougall Og, or their place holders, who are to

appoint a suitable man to take the place of Allan Cameron in respect of this contract, John Grant of Freuquhie also advising, etc.
Witnesses: John Grant of Freuquhie, William McIntosche of Essycht, Angus McIntosche in Termit, John Riach McCondochie, and Malcolm Ego, writer.
Mackintosh Muniments 187; NAS GD176/187

Appendix II

The Five Arrows of Clan Cameron

During the course of writing, I was invited by Donald Cameron of Lochiel XXVII to speculate on the significance of the Cameron crest of a sheaf of Five Arrows. Although only officially adopted as a heraldic crest in more recent times, the symbol of Five Arrows has been known within the clan for centuries. Today, the crest badge of Five Arrows encircled by the motto *Aonaibh Ri Chèil* enscribed on a strap-and-buckle is one of the most important symbols of clanship, held dear by Camerons the world over, and its historical significance is interpreted according to a statement written by the current chief's father, the late Colonel Sir Donald Cameron of Lochiel KT XXVI (1910-2004). In view of this, it is not without some trepidation that I offer my own thoughts on the possible origins of the symbol.

The earliest evidence known to the late Lochiel was from a snuffbox and pistol belonging to Donald 'the Gentle Lochiel' XIX (c.1700-1748), which confirm it was in existence before the Jacobite Rising of 1745, though it may of course go back to an earlier period. He wrote that, 'As regards the meaning of the five arrows, it definitely refers to the five branches of the clan, and I remember my father at a pre-war clan gathering mentioning this and stating which were the five branches concerned but, unfortunately, I have no record of what he actually said.' Lochiel went on to say that, according to what he had read, there seem to have been 'only five branches of any significance which were in existence before 1745, so I am sure these are the ones relating to the five arrows.'

Lochiel named these branches as:
1) MacMartins or Camerons of Letterfinlay
2) Camerons of Glen Nevis
3) Camerons of Callart and Lundavra
4) Camerons of Erracht
5) Camerons of Clunes

Lochiel's account has preserved the oral tradition that the arrows represent the five branches of the clan, and his position as hereditary chief of the clan greatly strengthens the authority of his testimony, constituting powerful evidence that this is indeed the traditional significance of the symbol. The second element of Lochiel's statement however does not have the authority of ancient tradition, and was apparently offered by him merely as a probable interpretation of received lore.

Thus, the late Lochiel's testimony begins with his recollection of the tradition that the Five Arrows badge refers to five branches of the clan, and continues with reasoned speculation as to the identity of the five families involved. The solution offered has a good deal to recommend it, but it is curious that the Camerons of Kinlochiel and indeed the Camerons of Lochiel themselves should be omitted, and it remains unclear why Clan Cameron should have adopted such an unusual symbol. It seems appropriate to look again at alternative answers to the riddle of the Five Arrows.

The meaning and purpose of the Five Arrows

The symbolism of the sheaf of arrows evokes a piece of timeless proverbial wisdom. According to Plutarch's *Moralia*, the Scythian king Scilurus offered a bundle of darts to each of his sons, asking them to break it. When none could break the bundle, he showed how each dart could easily be broken on its own, 'teaching them that, if they held together, they would continue strong, but if they fell out and were divided, they would become weak.'[118] Thus, the badge of Five Arrows is a symbol of strength in unity, echoed in the Cameron motto, *Aonaibh Ri Chèil*, 'Let Us Unite'.

Symbols of unity are most needed at times when such unity cannot easily be taken for granted. During the late seventeenth and early eighteenth centuries, the Cameron alliance was secure, and men from allied septs began to use the Cameron name. But in the early years of the chiefship of Allan McConnell Dow XVI, potential divisions within the clan were still all too real. For the first two decades of his chiefship, Allan's authority had been compromised by the continued presence of Donald McEwen Beg, and the clan once more came close to disintegration in 1612.

We have seen that Allan was not only ready to use violence to teach his followers 'in quhat forme they sall carye thame selffis to their Chief,' but that he combined this forcible assertion of his power with the reversal of his policy towards Clan Gregor to accommodate the political loyalties of his supporters. Allan knew that violence alone would not unite the clan, and he had seen that even his own kindred could turn against him. He and his clan needed something which might inspire his followers to unite.

There can rarely have been a time when Clan Cameron was more in need of a symbol of unity, and there can rarely have been a chief who staked more on maintaining that unity. So, although it may never be possible to demonstrate the truth of the matter one way or another, it seems reasonable to suggest that it was Allan McConnell Dow of Lochiel who first described the clan as a sheaf of five arrows, as part of his desperate but ultimately successful attempt to bring the clan together under his own leadership. Allan may have encountered Plutarch's image during his schooldays at Dunoon, where his schoolmaster was the father of Protestant theologian John Cameron (d.1625), who was known by the sobriquet 'The Walking Library' and was fluent in both Latin and Greek.[119]

Which families are represented by the Five Arrows?

If we assign one arrow to each of the various families of Cameron descent, we run out of arrows before reaching such long-standing traditional allies as the MacMartins and MacSorleys. To account for each and every branch of the Cameron line would require countless arrows, but if we limit ourselves only to lineages distinguished from the family of Lochiel by their own Gaelic designation, we do in fact arrive at five distinct groups, comprising the chiefly line of Lochiel under *Mac Dhòmhnaill Duibh,* and four cadet branches: Callart (*Sliochd Iain Mhic Ailein*); Erracht (*Sliochd Eoghainn Mhic Eoghainn*); Clunes (*Sliochd Iain Mhic Eoghain*); and Kinlochiel (*Sliochd Iain Dubh*). However, this still leaves some Camerons unaccounted for; we have used up all five arrows, yet have found no place not only for MacMartins or MacSorlies, but also for known individuals of lineal Cameron descent such as Donald McAllan VcEwen in Mamore who signed the 'Contract of Mutual Defence' in 1570. By this interpretation of the symbol, these outlying Camerons would seem to have been ignored and disenfranchised, yet if the Five Arrows symbol was indeed intended as a symbol of unity, it must surely have included all the families that rallied to the banner of Lochiel.

Looked at from another perspective, all these various Cameron lines are simply branches on the same Cameron family tree, and ultimately share the same roots and ancestry. To represent what is in reality a single family by several arrows could suggest division rather than unity. So, it might have been more politically meaningful if each arrow had symbolised a separate agnatic line, representing five unrelated families who had banded together in a mutual alliance.

According to this interpretation, all the descendants of the original Clan Cameron would be represented by a single arrow, alongside an arrow for the MacMartins of Letterfinlay and another for the MacSorleys of Glennevis. The two remaining arrows would then denote the two other families who formed a part of the Cameron alliance, *viz.* the MacGillonies of Strone, and the MacMillans of Murlaggan and Caillich. By putting all the arrows together in a single sheaf they are all accorded equal value so, to avoid getting into questions of precedence, they are given here in alphabetical order:

      I. Cameron
      II. MacGillonie of Strone
      III. MacMartin of Letterfinlay
      IV. MacMillan of Murlaggan and Caillich
      V. MacSorley of Glennevis and Dawnie

This still leaves out the MacPhees in Glendessary, but their status as tenants of Lochiel put them in a very different relationship to the other allied clans. The MacPhees arrived in Lochaber as broken men after the murder of their chief at the hands of Colkitto in 1623, at which date the symbolism of the Five Arrows may already have been established. As refugees without either lands or chief, the MacPhees were entirely dependent on Lochiel, so there may have been no need to acknowledge them with their own arrow. Likewise, the role of the

MacLachlans of Coruanan seems to have been based on a tradition of personal service as standard bearers to Lochiel, which distinguishes them from other more autonomous local septs. By contrast, the MacMartins, MacSorleys, MacMillans and MacGillonies all had landed chieftains of their own and, although in practice they were sometimes bound to Lochiel as his feudal vassals, they could in theory have chosen not to follow him had they so wished. The adoption of the Cameron name by these allied clans may have been part of the same deliberate statement of unity, which is expressed through the clan motto and emblem of Five Arrows.

Like any symbol, the Cameron badge of Five Arrows can bear multiple interpretations, and it may be significant that the original Cameron family line can itself be divided into five branches, each with its own Gaelic designation. Furthermore, a meaning which might have been apposite four hundred years ago may be less relevant today, so the current meaning for the clan need not be defined by historical analysis alone. However, if the speculation above is correct, the original symbolism behind the Five Arrows represents a powerful statement that, no matter which ancestral line a clansman or clanswoman may be descended from, it is loyalty to the clan which makes a Cameron.

Bibliography

I. Documentary sources

Argyll Papers, Inveraray
Argyll Transcripts, Volume VII

The Court of the Lord Lyon
Lyon Register, Volume 1

National Archives of Scotland, Edinburgh
NAS GD112/39/3/12, Breadalbane Muniments. Donald Dow, captain of the Clanchamberon, to Colin Campbell of Glenurquhay
NAS GD112/39/4/23, Breadalbane Muniments. Archibald, 5th earl of Argyll, Inneraray, to the laird of Glenurchay, his cousin
NAS GD112/39/5/21, Breadalbane Muniments. Ranald MacRenill of Keppoch to Colin Campbell of Glenuquhay
NAS GD112/39/6/2, Breadalbane Muniments. [Glenorchy to 'Gossip' John Campbell, Captain of Carrick]
NAS GD112/39/7/10, Breadalbane Muniments. [William Stewart of Grantully to Colin Campbell of Glenorchy]
NAS GD112/39/7/21, Breadalbane Muniments. John, 4th earl of Atholl, Blair in Atholl, to the laird of Glenurquhaye, his cousin
NAS GD112/39/8/4, Breadalbane Muniments. John, 4th earl of Atholl, Blair in Atholl, to the laird of Glenurquhay, his cousin
NAS GD112/39/8/6, Breadalbane Muniments. Ranald McRenill of Keppoch, The Keppoch, to the Earl of Atholl, his lord and master
NAS GD112/39/8/19, Breadalbane Muniments. [William Stewart of Grandtully to Glenorchy]
NAS GD112/39/9/2, Breadalbane Muniments. Donald McEvyn WicEvin in Lochaber to Colin Campbell of Glenurquhay

NAS GD112/39/9/10, Breadalbane Muniments. William Maitland of Lethington, Blair in Atholl, to the laird of Glenurquhay

NAS GD112/39/11/10, Breadalbane Muniments. William Stewart of Grantullye, Dunketh, to the [lady] of Glenurquhay

NAS GD112/39/12/8, Breadalbane Muniments. Grandtully to Glenorchy

NAS GD112/39/12/12, Breadalbane Muniments. John Campbell of Lawiris, Perthe, to the laird of Glenurquhay, his grandfather

NAS GD112/39/12/15, Breadalbane Muniments. Donald McEwyn Vic Evin in Lochaber, Rannocht, to Colin Campbell of Glenurquhay

NAS GD112/39/12/8, Breadalbane Muniments. William Stewart of Grandtully to Colin Campbell of Glenorchy

NAS GD176/74, Mackintosh Muniments. Bond of Assurance by Allan Camroun, Chief and Captain of Clan Chamroun

NAS GD176/85, Mackintosh Muniments. Crown Precept of Sasine by Mary, Queen of Scots, narrating the service of Lachlan Makintoische as heir to the deceased William Makintoische of Dunnachtan, his father, in the lands of Glenloy and Locharkaige.

NAS GD176/87, Mackintosh Muniments. Bond of Manrent by Martyne McDonquhie Vic Martyne (on being put to liberty) to Donald McEwin Vic Ewin

NAS GD176/102, Mackintosh Muniments. Letter of Gift by King James VI

NAS GD176/129, Mackintosh Muniments. Bond by Donald Makewin Vikconill in Manmoir.

NAS GD176/150, Mackintosh Muniments. Commission under the quarter seal to George, Earl of Huntly, Lord Gordon and Badenoch, Lachlan McIntosche of Dunnachtane, John Grant of Frewquhy, Sir Patrick Gordon of Auchindoun, knight, and Thomas Gordon of Cluny

NAS GD176/185, Mackintosh Muniments. Discharge by James Petrie, merchant burgess of Elgin, to Lachlan McIntosche of Dunnauchten, for all that he was due to him, except the price of a cloak given at his command to Donald McKewin, valued at £14, 5s

NAS GD176/187, Mackintosh Muniments. Heads of Agreement made at Forrachine, 8th July 1598, between Lachlan McIntosche of Dunnachteine and Allan Cambrone of Locheill

RPS 1661/1/406 (NAS PA2/27, f.58-61), Decreit [for] Lauchlan Mcintosh against Ewan Cameron

II. Publications

Adam, Frank & Innes of Learney, Sir Thomas 1952 *The Clans Septs and Regiments of the Scottish Highlands*. Edinburgh: W & A K Johnston.

Bateman, Meg & MacLeod, Wilson 2007 *Duanaire na Sracaire (Songbook of the Pillagers): Anthology of Scotland's Gaelic Verse to 1600*. Edinburgh: Birlinn.

Beveridge, J & Donaldson, G (eds.) 1957 *Register of the Privy Seal of Scotland*, Vol. VI. Edinburgh: Scottish Record Office.

Brown, Jennifer M. 1977 'The exercise of power' in *Scottish Society in the Fifteenth Century* ed. Jennifer M. Brown. London: Edward Arnold.

Brown, Keith M 1986 *Bloodfeud in Scotland: Violence, justice and politics in an Early Modern society*. Edinburgh: John Donald.

Burton, J H & Masson, D (eds.) 1878-98 *Register of the Privy Council of Scotland*, 1st Series. Edinburgh: Scottish Record Office.

Campbell of Airds, Alasdair 2002, *A History of Clan Campbell: From Flodden to the Restoration* (Vol.II). Edinburgh: Edinburgh University Press.

Cathcart, Alison 2006 *Kinship and Clientage: Highland Clanship 1451-1609*. Leiden: Brill.

Dodgshon, R. A. 1989 "Pretense of blude' and 'place of thair dwelling': the nature of highland clans, 1500-1745' in R. A. Houston (ed.) *Scottish Society 1500-1800*, p169-198. Cambridge: Cambridge University Press.

Dawson, Jane E A (ed.) 1997 *Campbell Letters 1559-1583*. Edinburgh: Scottish History Society.

Drummond of Balhaldie, John 1737 *Memoirs of Sir Ewen Cameron of Lochiell, Chief of the Clan Cameron: with an introductory account of the history and antiquity of that family and of the neighbouring clans*. Crawfurd, William & Pitcairn, Robert (eds.) 1842. Edinburgh: The Maitland Club.

Ewing, John Thor (ed.) 2016 *Clan Ewen, Some Records of its History: A new facsimile edition with notes and commentary*. Edinburgh: Welkin Books.

Fraser, Sir William 1883 *The Chiefs of Grant*, Vol.III. Edinburgh.

Fraser-Mackintosh, Dr Charles 1890-91 'Minor Highland Septs - No. IV. The Camerons of Letterfinlay, styled "Macmartin",' *Transactions of the Gaelic Society of Inverness*, Vol.XVII, p31-45. Inverness: The Gaelic Society of Inverness.

Goodare, Julian 1999 *State and Society in Early Modern Scotland*. Oxford: Oxford University Press.

Goodare, Julian 2004 *The Government of Scotland 1560-1625*. Oxford: Oxford University Press.

Gregory, Donald 1836 (1881) *History of the Western Highlands & Isles of Scotland, 1493-1625*. London: Hamilton, Adams & Co.

MacFarlane, Walter 1750-51 *Genealogical Collections concerning Families in Scotland, made by Walter MacFarlane 1750-51*. Clark, James Toshach (ed.) 1900. Edinburgh: Scottish History Society.

MacGibbon, David & Ross, Thomas 1889 *The Castellated and Domestic*

Architecture of Scotland from the twelfth to the eighteenth centuries, Vol.III. Edinburgh: David Douglas.

MacInnes, Allan 2008 'Lochaber - The last bandit country, c.1600-c.1750,' *Transactions of the Gaelic Society of Inverness*, Vol.LXIV. p1-21. Inverness: The Gaelic Society of Inverness.

MacGregor, Martin 1989 'A Political History of the MacGregors before 1571,' University of Edinburgh Ph.D. thesis.

MacKellar, Mary 1883 'To the Editor of The Celtic Magazine,' *The Celtic Magazine*, Vol.8, p268-74. Inverness: A & W Mackenzie.

Mackenzie, Alexander 1884 *History of the Camerons, with genealogies of the principal families of the name*. Inverness: A & W Mackenzie.

Mackenzie, Annie M. (ed.) 1964 *Òrain Iain Luim: Songs of John MacDonald Bard of Keppoch*, Scottish Gaelic Texts 8. Edinburgh: Scottish Gaelic Texts Society.

MacLeod, Wilson 2013 'Sovereignty, Scottishness and Royal Authority in Caimbeul Poetry of the Sixteenth Century' in *Fresche fontanis: Studies in the Culture of Medieval and Early Modern Scotland* edited by Janet Hadley Williams, J. Derrick McClure p231-48. Newcastle-upon-Tyne: Cambridge Scholars.

MacPhail, J. R. N. 1896 'Letters written by Mrs. Grant of Laggan concerning Highland affairs and persons connected with the Stuart cause in the eighteenth century' p249-330 in *Wariston's Diary and other Papers*, Publications of the Scottish History Society, Vol.XXVI. Edinburgh: Edinburgh University Press.

Martin, Martin (1703) 1716 *A Description of the Western Islands of Scotland*. London: A. Bell.

Meek, Donald (ed.) 1978 *The Campbell Collection of Gaelic Proverbs and proverbial Sayings*. Inverness: Gaelic Society of Inverness.

Newton, Michael 2009 *Warriors of the Word: The world of the Scottish Highlanders*. Edinburgh: Birlinn.

Nicolson, Alexander (1881) 1996 *A Collection of Gaelic Proverbs and familiar Phrases*. Edinburgh: Birlinn.

Pitcairn, Robert 1833 *Ancient Criminal Trials in Scotland*, Vol.I, Parts I & II. Edinburgh: The Bannatyne Club.

Roberts, John L. 1999 *Feuds, Forays and Rebellions: History of the Highland clans 1475-1625*. Edinburgh: Edinburgh University Press.

Stevenson, Joseph (ed.) 1883 *The History of Mary Stewart, by Claude Nau*. Edinburgh: W. Paterson.

Stewart of Ardvorlich, John 1974 (1981) *The Camerons: A history of Clan Cameron*. Glasgow: Clan Cameron Association.

Wormald, Jenny 1980 'Bloodfeud, Kindred and Government in Early Modern Scotland,' *Past and Present*, Vol.87, p54-97. Oxford: The Past and Present Society.

Wormald, Jenny 1985 *Lords and Men in Scotland: Bonds of Manrent, 1442-1603*. Edinburgh: John Donald.

Index

Allan McConnell Dow Cameron XII (d.1480), 32
Allan McConnell Dow Cameron XVI (d.1647), 12, 13-4, 15-7, 18-9, 27, 28, 30, 31, 36, 42-8, 52-3, n81, n95, n101, 62-4, (69), 80, 82-3, 86-7, Fig.2 (p23)
Appin, see 'Stewart of Appin'
Ardvorlich, John Stewart of, see 'Stewart of Ardvorlich'
Atholl, Earl of, see 'Stewart of Atholl'
Argyll, Earls of, see 'Campbell of Argyll'
Balhaldie, John Drummond of, see 'Drummond of Balhaldie'
bonds of manrent, see 'manrent'
Callart, Fig.1 (p8)
Callart and Lundavra, Camerons of (*Sliochd Iain Mhic Ailein*), 39-40, 85, 87, n62
Cameron, John (theologian, d.1625), 87
Cameron of Erracht, Allan (d.1828), 50-1
Campbell of Argyll, Archibald, 5th Earl of Argyll (d.1573), 22-6, 37-8, 74
Campbell of Argyll, Colin, 6th Earl of Argyll (d.1584), 41-2, 43-4, n83
Campbell of Argyll, Archibald, 7th Earl of Argyll (d.1638), 47
Campbell of Glenorchy, Colin (d.1583), 22-3, 25-6, 36-9, 41, 70-1, 73-6, n75, n90
Campbell of Lawers, John (d.c.1611) 38
Carberry Hill, 9, 25
Chase-About Raid, 22
Clunes, Camerons of (*Sliochd Iain Mhic Eoghain*), 85, 87; see also 'John Dow McEwen Cameron of Erracht'
Corrichie, Battle of, 21, 25
Disputed Lands, see 'Glen Loy and Loch Arkaig'
Donald McAllan VcEwen Cameron in Mamore, 34-5, 72-3, 87, n60
Donald Dow McConnell Cameron XV (d.1569), 12, 16-8, 19, 21-6, 27-31, 33, 35, 36, 37, 40-1, 44, 48, 51-3, 70, 77, n10, n15, n19, n24, n38, , Fig.2 (p23)
Donald Dow MacDonald (d.1545), 11
Donald Dow McEwen Cameron of Erracht (d.1570), 13, 18-20, 26-31, 33-5, 37-40, 43, 45-6, 48, 52, 62-3, 71, 74-6, 79, n19, n37, n62, n76, n90, n101, Fig.2 (p23)
Donald McEwen Beg '*An Taillear Dubh*' Cameron, 11-12, 13, 15-7, 30-1, 33-6, 39, 40-1, 43-7, 49, 53, 62-3, 64-70, 79, 81, 86, n76, n85, n90, Fig.2 (p23)
Donald McEwen Cameron (d.1538), 11, 14, 22, 64, n15, Fig.2 (p23)
Drummond of Balhaldie, John, (*Memoirs of Sir Ewen Cameron*), 12, 13-4, 15, 16, 17, 18, 19, 20, 21, 28, 30-1, 32, 34, 35, 36, 39, 40, 44, 46, 52, 62-4, n6, n7, n19, n21, n36, n42, n50, n54, n56, n82, n90, n92, n98, n106; (*Inventorie of the Charters*), n22

Dunstaffnage, 13, 44, 63, 69, n100
Dunoon, 42, 87
Erracht (place), 27, 39, Fig.1 (p8)
Ewen Beg McConnell Cameron XIV (d.1553), 11-2, 19, 28, n5, n9, n76, Fig.2 (p23)
Ewen McAllan Cameron XIII (d.1546), 10-11, 13, 14, 18, 19, 20, 22, 25, 32, 33, 34, 62, n5, n15, n24, n81, Fig.2 (p23)
Ewen McAne Cameron, Captain of Inverlochy, 39, 46, 77, 78, n81, n95
Ewen McEwen Cameron of Erracht (d. before 1567), 11, 18-20, 52, n5, n19, n37, n49, Fig.2 (p23)
feuding, 49-50
Glen Loy and Loch Arkaig, 25-6, 31-3, 71, Fig.1 (p8)
Glen Nevis, 22
Glennevis, MacSorleys or Camerons of, 22, 35, 46, 85, 88-9, n60
Gordon of Huntly, George, 4th Earl of Huntly (d.1562), 21-2
Gordon of Huntly, George, 5th Earl of Huntly (d.1576), 25
Gordon of Huntly, George, 1st Marquess of Huntly (d.1636), 47, 49, 82
Grandtully, see 'Stewart of Grandtully'
Grant of Freuchie, John (d.1585), 22, 30, 35, 53, 75
Gregory, Donald (*History of the Western Highlands and Isles of Scotland*), 14, 18-20, 51, n18, n37
Huntly, Earls of, see 'Gordon of Huntly'
Innis Chonnell, 12, 65, n9
Inverlochy, 13, 18, 39, 63, 69, n83
John Bodach McVcEwen Cameron of Erracht (d.1613), 46-8, n96
John Dow McEwen Cameron of Erracht, 13, 20, 24, 27-31, 33, 39-41, 43-6, 48, 50, 52, n96, Fig.2 (p23)
John Dow McEwen Cameron of Kinlochiel (d.1550), 16, 18-20, n15, n19, Fig.2 (p23)
John McAne Dow Cameron of Kinlochiel, 44, n100, Fig.2 (p23)
Kinlochiel, Fig.1 (p8)
Kinlochiel, Camerons of (*Sliochd Iain Dubh*), 13, 16, 19, 62, 69, 85, 87, n19; see also 'John Dow McEwen Cameron of Kinlochiel (d.1550)', 'John McAne Dow Cameron of Kinlochiel'
Lethington, see 'Maitland of Lethington'
Letterfinlay, 21, 28, Fig.1 (p8)
Letterfinlay, MacMartins or Camerons of, 26, 28, 46-7, 85, 88, n17; see also 'Martin McConaghy MacMartin of Letterfinlay'
Lindsay, Patrick, 6th Lord Lindsay of the Byres (d.1589), 29
Loch Arkaig, see 'Glen Loy and Loch Arkaig'
Loch Eil, 10, Fig.1 (p8)
Lordship of the Isles, 10-1, 41, 48

MacDonald Lords of the Isles, see 'Lordship of the Isles'
MacDonald of Clanranald, John (d.1584), 24, (40), (77)
MacDonald of Duniveg, James (d.1565), 11
MacDonald of Keppoch, Ranald Og (d.1587), 24, 37
MacDonald of Lochalsh, Alexander (d.1494), 10
MacDougall of Dunollie, John (d.1562), 11-2, 63-4, 69
Macewan of Glenboig, William, n96
MacFarlane, Walter (*Genealogical Collections*), 31, 71, n53, n103
MacGregor of Glenstrae, Gregor Roy (d.1570), 25, 36-7
MacKellar, Mary, 15-7, 18, 31, 33, 35, 36, 43, 45, 51, 64-70, n9, n11, n13, n16, n105, n107
Mackenzie, Alexander (*History of the Camerons*), 15, 18, n12, n19, n46, n47, n48
Mackintosh of Dunachton, Lachlan Mor (d.1606), 25-6, 31-3, 43-5, 47, 67-8, 77, 80-2, n32, n49
Mackintosh of Dunachton, William (d.1550), 11, 25, n32
Maclean of Duart, Hector Mor (d.1568), 12, 24
Maclean of Duart, Hector Og (d.1573), 42, n91
MacPhees in Glendessary, 88
Maith an Chairt Ceannas na nGaoidheal, 42, n93
Maitland of Lethington, William (d.1573), 38, 76
Mamore, 22, 34-5, 44, 80-1, 87, n60, Fig.1 (p8)
manrent, 26-7, 41, 44, 71, 79, 81, n34
Martin McConaghy MacMartin of Letterfinlay, 26, 28, 39, 65, n62
Martin, Martin (*A Description of the Western Islands*), 34
Mary, Queen of Scots (d.1587), 9, 22-6, 28-9, n32, n40
Memoirs of Sir Ewen Cameron, see 'Drummond of Balhaldie'
Moyness Raid (1598), 46, n109
Mucomir, 45, 68, Fig.1 (p8)
Murlaggan and Caillich, MacMillans of, 88-9
proverbs, 30, 34, 70, 86
Stewart of Grandtully, William (d.1575), 17, 38, 39, 71, 76, 81, n29
Stewart of Appin, John (d.c.1595), 24, 36-7, (64), (69), 73, n97
Stewart of Ardvorlich, John (*The Camerons*), 18, 19, 40, 44, 77, n1, n3, n19, n20, n22, n23, n39, n45, n46, n48, n54, n55, n59, n86, n99, n116, n117
Stewart of Atholl, John, 4th Earl of Atholl (d.1579), 24-6, 36-9, 40, 71, 73-4, 76, 78-9, n29, n75, n83, n97
Strone, 27, Fig.1 (p8)
Strone, MacGillonies or Camerons of, 88-9
Taillear Dubh, see 'Donald McEwen Beg'
tanistry, 11, n5
Tor Castle, 27, Fig.1 (p8)
tutor, 13-4, 16, 18-9, 22, 27, 28, 30-2, 34-6, 40, 43-4, 51-3, 62-3, 73, n19

www.ingramcontent.com/pod-product-compliance
Lightning Source LLC
LaVergne TN
LVHW091109080426
835508LV00009B/892